Prairie Cooks

A Bur Oak

Original

Prairie Cooks

GLORIFIED RICE,
THREE-DAY BUNS,
AND OTHER REMINISCENCES

BY CARRIE YOUNG
WITH FELICIA YOUNG

University of Iowa Press   Iowa City

University of Iowa Press,
Iowa City 52242
Copyright © 1993 by
Ahdele Carrine Young
and Felicia C. Young
Printed in the United States
of America

Some of the recipes in this book
were originally published in the
author's articles for *Gourmet*,
entitled "A Prairie Cook" and
"A Scandinavian Thanksgiving
in North Dakota." Copyright ©
1983 *Gourmet*. Reprinted by
permission. "Glorified Rice"
appeared originally in the cen-
tennial issue of *North Dakota
Quarterly* 56, no. 4, 1988.

Printed on acid-free paper

97 96 95 94 93 C 5 4 3 2 1

Scratchboard illustration by
Beth Krommes

Library of Congress
Cataloging-in-Publication Data
Young, Carrie.
   Prairie cooks: glorified rice,
three-day buns, and other
reminiscences / by Carrie Young
with Felicia Young.
      p.   cm. — (A Bur oak
original)
   Includes index.
   ISBN 0-87745-436-1 (cloth)
   1. Cookery, Norwegian.
2. Norwegian Americans—
North Dakota—Food.
3. Norwegian Americans—
North Dakota—Social life and
customs.   I. Young, Felicia.
II. Title.   III. Series.
TX722.N6Y68 1993 93-17414
641.59481—dc20   CIP

FOR THE BERG GIRLS

Barney

Florence

Gladys

Fran

Peggy

AND FOR NORMAN

the brother who put up with them

Preface

Lucky are we who can look back on our childhoods and remember with pleasure the unique taste and aroma of our mothers' cooking.

I grew up, the youngest of six children, on my parents' homestead farm in North Dakota in the years before, during, and after the Dust Bowl. My recall of the harshest of these years is mitigated by the goodness of my mother's food and that of her neighbors. These homestead wives, most of them daughters of Scandinavian immigrants, knew how to "make do," and they made do very well, indeed. Despair was never so great that it couldn't be pushed back by coffee and *fattigman* fresh from the lard kettle at four o'clock in the afternoon.

Because of circumstances, my mother had an ongoing involvement with the preparation of food for most of her life. Born in Norway in 1879, my mother came to this country at the age of three with her parents and siblings. They settled on a Minnesota farm. Her own mother, of course, brought her children up on Norwegian cooking. When my mother was fifteen, she was sent to "work out" in the home of a Sauk Center family. She moved on to Minneapolis, where she worked for almost ten years as a cook and housekeeper in the home of a well-to-do family and became an accomplished cook of what she always called "American" food.

But she never forgot the taste of her mother's Norwegian cooking, and after she homesteaded in western North Dakota and later married another homesteader of Norwegian heritage, she quickly took up Scandinavian cooking again, blending it with the "American" style she had learned in Minneapolis. She was determined that her own children should enjoy the customs and food of the Old Country. In turn, my sisters and I passed down to our children the old Scandinavian recipes. My own daughter has always been captivated with her Norwegian heritage. She and I have collaborated on this book of recipes and reminiscences; she compiled and tested the recipes, and I have contributed the reminiscences.

—Carrie Young

Prairie Cooks

1. *L*utefisk and *L*efse

No immigrants have become more ardent and patriotic Americans than the Norwegian homesteaders. On the other hand, no group has held on to its Old World customs more fiercely. As the twentieth century draws to its close, those of us who are their children and grandchildren and great grandchildren cling tenaciously to the traditions they passed down to us almost a hundred years ago. This attitude is reflected in the unabashed enthusiasm with which we continue to espouse Scandinavian foods and festivals.

Williams County, North Dakota, where I grew up, is a typical Norwegian-American settlement that continues to

My mother, Carrine Gafkjen, right, and her sister Carrie, in turn-of-the-century Minneapolis. They had sewn every stitch of these beautiful dresses themselves by hand. From the author's collection.

become prouder of its heritage with each year. The vast majority of the homesteaders who came here were either Norwegian immigrants themselves or the sons and daughters of immigrants who had settled in eastern North Dakota, Minnesota, or Wisconsin a generation earlier. My mother was born in Hallingdal, Norway, and shortly afterward came to Minnesota with her parents. My father was born in eastern North Dakota, but his parents also had emigrated from Norway—from Hallingdal, in fact. When he and my mother met in Williams County after both had homesteaded, it was easy to see why they were attracted to each other! They are a good example of how sons and daughters of immigrants met as pioneers in the new country and formed what they considered the perfect union.

Listening to Norwegian-Americans in Williams County talk about food, one can easily get the impression that *lutefisk* and *lefse* are the be-all and end-all; it just doesn't get any better than this. I agree wholeheartedly that it doesn't get any better than *lefse*. But *lutefisk*?

An old Norwegian dictionary of mine defines *lutefisk* as "codfish steeped in lye of potash." The sound of these words may be an indication of its palatability.

Still, I would be the last person to run down *lutefisk*; I ingested it every Thanksgiving and Christmas from early childhood on up with not a word of protest. There was never a peep out of my five siblings, either. (One or two of them actually liked it.) Loyal children of Norwegian immigrants do not raise the hand of treason against the homeland.

The most important job my father had in preparing for the winter holidays was to go to Appam, the small town five miles north of us, and buy the *lutefisk* before the grocer had to reach too far down in the barrel.

Lutefisk was conceived in Scandinavia centuries ago, when the customary way to preserve fish was to dry it out. We can only theorize that one morning a rugged Norseman may have awakened betimes, in some lonely outpost, craving fresh fish instead of the dried fish he had been subsisting on for days. Suddenly an ingenious idea came to him out of his desperation. He soaked his dried codfish until it had taken on all the water it could handle. Then he steeped it for days in a lye of potash. Then he rinsed the lye out. He ended up with a heavy white mass that looked and smelled like fish. Eureka! *Lutefisk* was born.

When the earliest Norwegian immigrants came to the United States they also had to make *lutefisk* themselves, but it was a long and tortuous process. As the years went by and states such as North Dakota, Minnesota, and Wisconsin became heavily populated with Scandinavians, the meat and fish packers acceded to demand and began to process *lutefisk* themselves for shipping to their retail outlets during the winter months. Most of the *lutefisk* made in the United States today is processed by half a dozen food companies who sell well over a million tons annually. They even put it up in pouches suitable for the microwave.

Perhaps one reason *lutefisk* remains so popular among the descendants today is this: the ability to consume it in great quantities and with enormous gusto during the holidays and ethnic celebrations is not only a sign that we still have Viking blood coursing through our veins, but it is a symbolic tribute to our hardy ancestors who braved the New World to find a better life.

LUTEFISK

Rinse *lutefisk* thoroughly in several salted waters, then remove loose dark skin and fins and cut in serving-size pieces. Because the fish is delicate, it will retain its shape better if placed in cheesecloth before putting it in a large shallow pan. Cover with more cold salted water. Bring to a gentle boil, turn heat down, and simmer for about 5 minutes or until fish is tender and translucent. Place on serving platter and cover with drawn or clarified butter.

Clarified Butter

Place a stick of butter in a small saucepan over low heat. When melted remove from heat and let stand for a few minutes until milk solids have settled to bottom. Skim butter from top and place in pitcher.

As far as *lutefisk*'s traditional companion, *lefse*, is concerned, I don't think there is anything obligatory in our willingness to consume it in great amounts during holidays. *Lefse* is as satisfactory a morsel of food as anyone— even a non-Norwegian—could ask for. Although it is often described as a potato pancake, it is much more versatile than a pancake, and, like bread, it is a suitable accompaniment for any meal. Our mothers and grandmothers baked it directly on top of their cast-iron cookstoves, in round sheets some 24 inches in diameter. Memories of our childhoods are more pleasant because of it.

My mother and her neighbors spent many hours making *lefse* for the winter holidays. The ingredients are simple: good creamy mashed potatoes thickened with flour to rolling consistency. But the way our mothers made it was not as simple as it sounds. After they had rolled the huge circle of dough very thin on their pastry boards, they had to roll it halfway up again on a long *lefse* stick and carry it to the cookstove to be unrolled. Unless just the right amount of flour had been incorporated into the potatoes, the *lefse* would come apart during its journey to the stove, or it would stick to itself and refuse to be unrolled on top of the range. The first piece of *lefse* was usually sacrificial.

The women in our small farm community each made such distinctive *lefse* that you could almost close your eyes, take a bite, and tell who had baked it. My mother's *lefse* was very rich with butter and cream, and it came off the range still rather moist inside. Some of the women liked theirs thicker or thinner or drier or browner. One or two even put sugar in, which my mother thought was a sin. My Uncle Ole's wife, Anna, who lived across the road, made *lefse* that could only be called exquisite. Like everything else she did, it had to be perfect. It was flaky and pale and perfectly flecked in all the right places. She was so fussy about it and it took her so long that she didn't make it very often; when she gave you a piece of it you knew you were getting something special, and you'd better make it last a while.

I prefer to make mine the simple way, in manageable circles on my 10-inch cast-iron pancake griddle. Following is a small but very specific recipe for *lefse*, which my mother worked up for me after I married and established my own household. If followed exactly, it duplicates—in miniature—the taste of my mother's *lefse*.

LEFSE

2½ pounds (6 to 8) boiling potatoes	2 tablespoons milk
¼ cup butter	2 teaspoons salt
2 tablespoons light cream	¼ teaspoon pepper
	1 cup flour

Peel and boil 6 to 8 potatoes until very tender; drain, mash, and measure 4 cups. (Reserve the water for making potato bread, if desired; see page 63). Add butter, cream, milk, salt, and pepper, and mash again until very creamy. Chill lightly covered with waxed paper or cloth 2 to 4 hours or until well chilled. Add the cup of flour to the dough and work in well with hands. (Do not add flour before you refrigerate. *Lefse* must be made immediately after flour is added.)

It will be much easier to roll *lefse* if you use a pastry cloth and a stocking on your rolling pin which have been well seasoned with flour from previous use. Measure ¼ cup of dough, form it in a ball, and put it on the pastry cloth on which 1 tablespoon of flour has been spread. Roll dough to a 7- or 8-inch circle. If dough is sticky and comes apart when rolling, gather it together, add another tablespoon of flour to the pastry cloth, and try again.

Heat a well-seasoned cast-iron griddle. Do not grease. If you have an electric burner with eight settings, a No. 3 is just right for *lefse*—but better to have the heat too low than too high. Using a wide metal spatula or *lefse* stick, if you have one, lift the circle of *lefse* up from the pastry cloth on one side, using your other hand to help lift it on the other side, and carry it to the griddle. Prick the dough in four or five places with the corner of the spatula. Let it bake for about a minute or until it bubbles in the middle, turn it carefully, and cook it for 45 seconds on the other side. If the heat is correct, it should still be very pale, with just a few flecks of brown. Turn again, then keep decreasing the turning time until you are turning about every 5 seconds, for a total of about 3 minutes. When done it should be dry on both sides but still tender and pliable; it should be pale brown flecked. Remove *lefse* to a dry dish towel and let cool. Wipe griddle with dry cloth between each *lefse*.

When cool, the circles can be piled up on each other. Store in a covered tin, overnight if desired, until ready to serve. To serve, halve them, spread with soft butter, and roll into cone-shaped rolls. Arrange the *lefse* on a decorative platter and serve as bread. *Lefse* freezes beautifully. It can be made several weeks ahead for special occasions. Just place in plastic bags and freeze. Then thaw several hours before serving at room temperature. Serves 6 to 8.

All year around Williams County Norwegians find some way of connecting with their roots. The most ongoing link is Bjarne Lodge 86 of the Sons of Norway, whose members meet the second Thursday of every month. One of 375 Sons of Norway lodges in thirty states and Canada, Bjarne Lodge was organized in 1908. An auxiliary, Daughters of Norway, with the name "Signe," was also organized. Women's liberation must have been a forerunner in Williams County, because in 1920 the Daughters of Norway were invited to unite with the Sons of Norway. Although Norwegian men have always been uncommonly efficient at preparing *lutefisk*, they have never been known for their skill with the *lefse* stick; perhaps this was a consideration.

At any rate, united and happy together, the Bjarnes and the Signes, like all of the other Sons of Norway lodges today, share good food, old songs, folk dances, genealogies, and trips back and forth to the Old Country. They all are devoted to charitable works. Bjarne Lodge bought Liberty Bonds in World War I, War Bonds in World War II, and helped build and remodel two hospitals. It regularly makes contributions to the Sons of Norway Foundation, the Vindland Center, Ski for Light, district scholarships, and language camps.

The frigid North Dakota winters are brightened considerably the third week of February, when the First Lutheran church in Williston stages its famous *Lutefisk* Dinner. This has been going on for sixty years. It takes 600 Norwegian-Lutherans to plan, prepare, and serve over 3,000 people who stand in long lines from 11 A.M. until 7 P.M. or "until the food is gone." They consume 3,000 pounds of *lutefisk* (note: this is a pound apiece for every man, woman, and child!), 700 pounds of *lefse*, 700 pounds of boiled potatoes to go with the *lutefisk*, and 700 pounds of mashed potatoes to go with the 600 pounds of Norwegian meatballs and gravy.

After this gargantuan feast, appetites for things Norse are somewhat sated until Syttende Mai, Norway's Independence Day on the seventeenth of May. In my early childhood, Syttende Mai was the day the men would go to town and lift their glasses to the glory of the Old Country while the women stayed home and waited patiently—or not so patiently—for their return; but in recent years Syttende Mai has re-emerged as the day when all Norwegians, women and men alike, reconfirm their pride in their ancestry. In the county seat of Williston, it is more like a victory celebration. The Norwegian flag is hoisted, waving in tandem with the Stars and Stripes. The women break out their *bunads*—their intricately embroidered Norwegian costumes—and there is Norwegian folk dancing in the streets. The banks serve coffee and pastries, and in generous years they have even been known to give a half percentage more on their CDs that day. (The Irish not excluded!) People walk up and down the streets shaking hands and greeting each other with "*Hausen gär det?*" How goes it?

When Syttende Mai is over, things ethnic calm down a bit during the summer, because *lutefisk* and *lefse* are traditionally cold-weather foods. Williams County Norwegians are quite content to eat "American" until the Samlingfest rolls around in late September in the tiny town of Zahl, thirty-five miles or so to the north of Williston. Zahl boasts a population of anywhere from nineteen to thirty-seven, depending on what year it is, to whom you are talking, and whether you count dogs and other itinerants.

Samlingfest means, simply, "We gather together." Started in 1982 by half a dozen or so vigorous women who were determined to put Zahl back on the map, they spent weeks planning a Scandinavian Food Fair and cajoling local entertainers to put on a stage show in an old abandoned schoolhouse. The first year hundreds came, the next, thousands. Now in its eleventh year, a *lutefisk* and *lefse* dinner is served, and food booths are set up for "buy and take home," which include every kind of Norwegian pastry known. Strolling clowns sell balloons printed with "Welcome to Samlingfest," and everywhere there are signs proclaiming "*Vær så god,*" which means "Be so good as to accept what we have to offer." Arts and crafts are displayed, with rosemaling and quilts for sale. The day ends with the stage show and dancing at the new community hall, paid for in part by Samlingfest.

In the middle of October, many Williams County Norwegians travel 125 miles east to the *Norsk Høstfest* in Minot, which was started in 1978 and was an instant and smashing success. It has been going strong every year since, featuring not only food but big-name musical performers, genealogy sessions, and numerous arts and crafts exhibits.

Many other Nordic festivals are held throughout the country. One of the largest and most comprehensive is the Nordic Fest at Decorah, Iowa. It has been holding forth annually for twenty-seven years and represents the best in Scandinavian culture, including artists, musicians, and dancers from the United States, Canada, and Norway. Decorah is also home to the Vesterheim (Western Home) Museum, North America's largest ethnic museum. It graphically depicts the saga of our Norse ancestors who left the Old World to start a new life in America.

As the year draws to a close and the weather gets colder and colder, the Viking blood of Williams Countians is reinvigorated, especially with the great feast festivals of Thanksgiving and Christmas looming ahead. Sandwiched in between these holidays is the annual First Lutheran Bake Sale the first or second week in December. This sale has been going on since 1928. The week before the sale, the women come to the church kitchens with their electric *lefse* griddles and their *lefse* sticks. One day they make two hundred pounds of *lefse*, and the next day they make another hundred pounds of *flatbrød*, all of which they pack into one-pound boxes. Other women are at home baking cookies, cakes, and pastries by the dozens, which they bring to the church. The sale begins at 2 P.M., by which time there is a long line surrounding the church. When the bell rings to signal the start of the sale, pandemonium breaks loose. In an hour or two, no matter how much the women bake, everything is gone. The tables are bare.

FLATBRØD

Flatbrød is a thin, crisp version of *lefse* made with buttermilk and whole wheat flour instead of potatoes and cream. Not as gutsy or as filling as *lefse*, it is more of a snack food. Homesteaders' wives baked it in large round sheets on top of their cast-iron stoves, just as they did their *lefse*. Their children and grandchildren make it on their electric *lefse* griddles. It takes even heat to crisp up the edges, so if you don't own an electric griddle, you're better off baking it on a large round pizza pan in the oven, which works well, except that you must open the oven door several times to turn the *flatbrød*.

¾ cup buttermilk	¼ cup sugar
¼ cup water	¾ teaspoon soda
7 tablespoons butter or	1 teaspoon salt
margarine	additional whole wheat
1¾ cups white flour	flour (for rolling out
1 cup whole wheat flour	flatbrød)
1 cup oatmeal	

In a small saucepan heat buttermilk and water together until very warm. Remove from heat, add butter, and stir until melted. Cool to lukewarm. Place white flour, ½ cup of the whole wheat flour, oatmeal, and other dry ingredients together in a large mixing bowl. Add liquid to it and mix well. Add the remaining ½ cup whole wheat flour and stir until it is just combined.

Place 1 level tablespoon of wheat flour on a pastry cloth, measure out ⅓ cup of dough, and pat it into a 2-inch round. With a rolling pin that has a well-seasoned sleeve, roll out the dough into a very thin 10-inch round (dough will be sturdy and elastic) using firm strokes. Trim any uneven edges with a pastry wheel. Using a *lefse* stick or wide spatula, transfer the round onto a griddle or baking sheet (a 12-inch round pizza pan is ideal). If using a griddle, turn circle every minute or so until light brown and crisp throughout, or about 5 minutes. If baking, place in the middle of a 325 degree oven. Bake for 4 minutes on one side, turn with spatula, and bake 5 minutes on the other side, then turn again and bake another 2 to 3 minutes until *flatbrød* looks evenly crisp. Transfer to a dish towel to cool. (*Flatbrød* will crisp up even more the first couple of minutes of cooling.) Make remaining rounds in the same way, always adding an additional 1 tablespoon wheat flour to the pastry cloth.

When cool and crisp, each circle can be broken into six or eight pieces and spread liberally with butter for snacking. Makes 8 or 9 10-inch rounds.

2. Cooking for the Threshers

In the early 1900s the owners of the large threshing rigs in western North Dakota were desperate to find cooks who would both work and live in the cook cars that were moved from homestead to homestead, which were often miles apart. In later years, each farmwife would cook for the threshers as they came along, but in the early years many of the homesteaders were still bachelors and were themselves part of the threshing crews.

There were scarcely any women in the territory who were willing or able to take on the almost around-the-clock job of cooking for two or three dozen men. My mother was one of these women. After she had proved up her homestead, she rented out her 160 acres on cropshares to a neighboring homesteader. In the winter she worked as a housekeeper for a well-to-do farm family in eastern North Dakota, but every summer for the next eight years she came back to her homestead and cooked for the threshers. She was more than up to the job; she had been cooking for large families since she was fifteen. Although most of the threshing rigs employed two cooks, she preferred to do the job alone and was paid one-and-a-half times the going wage, which, because of supply and demand, was sky high. The last year she cooked she was paid double—an unheard-of four dollars a day! At the end of that year she had saved enough money from her wages, along with the income from her crops, to buy outright another quarter section of land adjacent to her homestead.

The cook car in which my mother worked was similar in shape to a Pullman kitchen. Tin-roofed as a fire preventive, it had a coal-burning stove in a corner near the door. The flunky, the equivalent of the modern gofer, filled the coal buckets when he brought coal for the engine. While there, he also took out the ashes. In the other corner stood a barrel of water, filled daily by the water haulers who brought water for the steam engine. Against one wall was a worktable with a built-in metal rolling board. A metal safe held perishables such as meat, milk, eggs, and butter. Tremendous supplies were stacked in the rear, including hundred-pound sacks of flour, sugar, and potatoes. A bed hinged to the wall could be lowered for my mother to sleep on, but some nights she didn't bother to lower it, if her stove wasn't drawing and she had to bake bread all night. Against the other wall was a long narrow table with benches behind it, where eight or ten crewmen could eat at a time. First come, first served, and the others could take their plates and eat outside.

My mother always had half a dozen things going at once.

Bread was either setting, rising, or baking around-the-clock. She made twelve loaves at once. Always on the stove was a huge black kettle of lard in which she fried hundreds of doughnuts each day. She made pies with whatever the rig owners brought her: fresh or dried apples, rhubarb, raisins, lemons from the country groceries. They bought some of their perishable supplies such as milk, butter, eggs, meat, and garden vegetables from nearby homesteads.

On nights my mother managed to get any sleep at all, she had to get up at three in the morning to stir up the fire and get it hot enough to boil a couple of gallons of coffee and to make stacks of pancakes on the griddle that covered two holes on the range. She wanted to stockpile a quantity of pancakes to put in the warming oven so that she was ahead of the game before the men started coming in at first light. Otherwise the men could eat faster than she could fry. The water haulers and the fireman came in first, followed by a couple of the bundle-team drivers who would start picking up the first shocks in the field.

By sunrise, the entire crew had been fed and were out in the field, and she heard the first blast of the steam engine. My mother said she always timed her work by its sound. She loved to hear its rhythmic beat. If it suddenly stopped in the middle of the day, she knew there was a breakdown or a thunderstorm had come up and work would be delayed.

When she heard the steam engine going at its steady beat, she knew it was time to start frying doughnuts for forenoon lunch. By nine she had a dishpan filled with doughnuts and sandwiches ready to go out to the field. The flunky came to help her carry the tremendous granite coffeepot and the tin cups. She stood in the field near the threshing rig to pour the coffee. She was always careful to stand upwind from the blower so the straw dust didn't blow into the cups! The men came in relays as their wagons were emptied.

The threshing crew for which my mother cooked. Rig owners Tom Swenson and Theodore Helgeson stand at far left. My father, Sever Berg, is kneeling at first left. My mother's face is visible in the window. From the author's collection.

Then it was back to the cook car to prepare the noon dinner. If the threshers were working against the clock she would take dinner to the field, too—often a big pot of beef stew with potatoes, onions, and carrots. She always took pie to the field, because it carried well and was filling. She'd take four or five whole pies and serve them up on the tin plates after the men had finished their stew. The men loved her pies most of all, and lemon meringue was their favorite. They'd take small helpings of stew and go

for two pieces of pie. My mother had a magic touch with pie crusts. She could take any kind of shortening she had on hand, lard or butter, and get an incredibly flaky pastry every time.

After dinner, it was back to the lard kettle for more doughnuts for afternoon lunch. If she hadn't had to take dinner to the field and she had the time, she'd make *fattigman*, the diamond-shaped deep-fried Norwegian cookie. The problem here was that each member of the crew could eat half a dozen at a time without blinking, so it was often too time-consuming to make the quantity she needed. The nice thing about doughnuts was that they were very filling.

At four o'clock she had the afternoon lunch ready to go out to the field. The dishpan again filled with sandwiches, doughnuts and/or cookies, and a fresh pot of coffee. Every day my mother saved the eggshells she had used in baking and crushed them in with the ground coffee. Sometimes, if she could spare the whole egg, she put that in, too. It softened the water and made the coffee clear.

When she heard the steam engine go off at sundown, she knew the men would be straggling in for supper. She had made use of all the leftovers she had from the noon meal. Any leftover beef or pork from roasts or steaks she had ground up with the potatoes and vegetables, put it all in a small dishpan, moistened it with water, and had baked hash. She'd have biscuits alongside and a loaf cake.

After the last man had left it was time to light her lantern, hang it from the ceiling, and wash all of those tin plates, cups, and forks that had accumulated. Bread was still baking in the oven against the next day, and preparations must start for breakfast. Sift the flour for pancakes, slice bacon if there was any. Take the coffeepot outside and jettison the grounds. Grind fresh coffee. If the rig was going to move the next morning at first light, she would need to pack everything breakable.

As midnight neared she stood in the doorway of the cook car, breathing the fresh night air and looking at the dazzling North Dakota sky, where the stars met the horizon. She heard the plaintive sound of a mouth organ coming from the wagons where the men were bedded down. A horse staked out in the field whinnied, and another one answered it. She went back in and took the last loaves of bread out of the oven. She pulled her bed down from the wall, wondering if it was worth the effort to undress when she would be getting up in three hours to rekindle the fire in the stove. She put a couple of pieces of coal in and hoped she'd still have a few embers in the morning.

The last summer my mother worked in the cook car the young man who fired the steam engine always seemed to be the first one in for breakfast. He had eyes as blue and clear as the North Dakota sky at its most brilliant. He was a finicky eater. He always left something on his plate. Much of the time it was her pie crust. This wasn't easy for her to take. But he did speak Halling like nobody's business. She was lonesome for Halling, the dialect of the region in Norway in which she was born. He had a homestead, too, and he said he was so fond of it nothing could ever make him leave it. She told him that she felt the same way about her own homestead. She married him on New Year's Eve in 1912. They lived on his homestead for a year, and the next year they moved to hers. It was a measure of how much he loved her.

THRESHERS' STEW

2 pounds beef stew meat	For the gravy:
1/4 cup butter (for browning meat)	3 tablespoons flour
	3 cups water
1 large onion, sliced	1 1/2 teaspoons salt
6 large carrots, cut in chunks	1/2 teaspoon pepper
	1/2 teaspoon allspice

Shake stew meat in a paper bag with enough flour to cover. Brown meat in the 1/4 cup butter in a heavy frying pan together with the onion. Place meat in heavy saucepan.

Measure grease remaining in frying pan and if necessary add more butter to make 3 tablespoons. Add 3 tablespoons flour and stir over low heat until flour is browned. Add 3 cups water, salt, pepper, and allspice to make a rich brown gravy. Add gravy to the meat in saucepan and let simmer, covered, for 1 hour. Add carrots and let simmer 45 minutes longer (remove cover last 30 minutes). If gravy gets too thick during the cooking process, add more water. Serve with plenty of boiled or mashed potatoes. Serves 6.

SMULTBOLLER
(Sour Cream Doughnuts)

Because my mother thought that doughnuts were what kept an outdoor man from starving between meals—if brought to him in quantity with plenty of strong coffee—her doughnuts are truly macho.

2 large eggs	½ teaspoon salt
¾ cup sugar	½ teaspoon ground
1 teaspoon vanilla	cardamom
1 cup sour cream	granulated sugar (for
3¼ cups all-purpose flour	coating doughnuts, if
1 teaspoon soda	desired)
1 teaspoon baking powder	

In a large bowl beat together the eggs, sugar, and vanilla until the mixture is thick and pale, add the sour cream and combine well. Add all at once 3 cups of the flour that have been sifted with the remaining dry ingredients and stir the dough until it is just combined.

Turn dough out on a pastry cloth and use the remaining ¼ cup of flour, if needed, to roll out a smooth dough. Roll out to a good ⅝ inch thick and cut out as many rounds as possible with a floured 3-inch doughnut cutter and, if necessary, cut out the centers with a 1¼-inch cutter dipped in flour.

Gather the scraps into a ball and reroll the dough, then cut out as many more doughnuts as possible in the same manner. Cut out holes from any remaining scraps with the 1¼-inch cutter. After cutting, flatten the doughnuts just a little with the rolling pin to make larger than ordinary doughnuts.

Deep fry in several inches of oil at 375 degrees. Turn only once and fry a full 1½ minutes on either side or until golden brown. With a slotted spatula, transfer doughnuts and holes as they are fried to paper towels to drain. While they are still quite warm, if desired, shake the doughnuts in a paper bag of the granulated sugar, shaking off the excess. Serve warm or at room temperature. Makes 8 to 10 doughnuts and a dozen doughnut holes.

BUTTERMILK BISCUITS

2 cups all-purpose flour	1 teaspoon soda
2 teaspoons sugar	⅔ cup buttermilk
⅓ cup butter or margarine	

Sift flour and sugar together. Add butter and cut in as if mixing a pie crust. Stir soda into buttermilk and add all at once to flour mixture. Stir with a fork until it holds together. Turn out on floured board and knead two or three times. Pat dough into a 1-inch-high round and cut out with a 1½-inch biscuit cutter. Gently bunch any remaining dough to form and cut last biscuits. Place closely together on buttered baking sheet and brush tops lightly with buttermilk. Bake at 400 degrees for 10 to 15 minutes or until brown. Makes 16 to 18 biscuits.

NORTH DAKOTA
LEMON MERINGUE PIE

How the threshing crew loved my mother's lemon meringue pie! It was their favorite, a glorious tangy confection in that incredibly flaky crust they could put on their tin plates after they had finished their dinners to give them the feeling they were getting something extra special. My mother was always begging the owner of the threshing rig not to forget the lemons when he was foraging for supplies. It was one of the easiest pies she could make, because she could bake the crusts while she was boiling the filling, then she could fill the pie shells, spoon on the meringue, put the pies back in the oven for a few minutes and they were ready.

For the 9-inch baked pie shell: use recipe for Carrine's Flaky Pie Crust (see page 23)

For the filling:
1 cup sugar
1/4 cup cornstarch

1/2 teaspoon salt
1/3 cup fresh lemon juice
2 tablespoons grated lemon peel
3 large egg yolks
1 tablespoon butter
1 1/2 cups boiling water

In a heavy saucepan combine the sugar, cornstarch, salt, lemon juice, and lemon peel. Add the unbeaten egg yolks one at a time and beat well. Add the butter and the boiling water in a stream and, stirring constantly with a wooden spatula, bring the mixture to a boil. Simmer and continue to stir and cook for 3 minutes until the filling is thick, glossy, and transparent. Remove from heat, beat another minute, and pour into baked pie shell. Top with Meringue Topping.

Meringue Topping

3 large egg whites, at room temperature
1/2 teaspoon vanilla

1/4 teaspoon cream of tartar
1/4 teaspoon salt
1/4 cup sugar

In a large bowl with an electric mixer beat the egg whites with the vanilla, cream of tartar, and salt added until it holds soft, glossy peaks. Add sugar a tablespoon at a time and continue beating until it holds thick, stiff peaks. Tip bowl, slide rubber spatula under and around meringue to loosen, and slide onto pie all in one piece. Seal meringue to edges of pie, covering the filling and crust completely. Bake the pie in the middle of a 350 degree oven for 12 to 15 minutes until the meringue is golden brown. Let pie cool on a rack. Serves 8.

CARRINE'S FLAKY PIE CRUST
(for 9-inch pie shell)

1¼ cups all-purpose flour
¾ teaspoon salt
¼ cup stick butter, cut in
  pieces
3 tablespoons cold lard
  (margarine can be
  substituted)

3 tablespoons ice water
1 tablespoon softened
  butter

Put the flour and salt in a bowl with the butter and lard. Blend flour lightly into butter and lard between thumb and fingertips (or use a pastry cutter) until most of the flour has been absorbed and the mixture resembles coarse meal. Do not overblend. Sprinkle the 3 tablespoons ice water over the dough, toss lightly with a fork, and roll the dough around the bowl to take up the remaining flour. Form into a ball, put on pastry cloth on which a little flour has been sprinkled, and pat into a 6-inch circle. Spread the 1 table-spoon softened butter on the circle with a knife. Fold the dough in half and fold the halved dough again to form a pie-shaped wedge. Press the edges together and re-form the dough into a ball. Roll out ⅛ inch thick into a round 2 inches bigger than the inverted 9-inch pie tin. Fold dough in half to lift into pie pan, then unfold and ease crust into tin. Fold edges under and crimp with tines of a fork. Prick the shell lightly with the fork in several places and bake in a 400 degree oven for 15 to 20 minutes until it is puffed lightly and golden. Cool on rack while making filling.

DAKOTA POUND CAKE

1 cup butter or margarine plus 2 tablespoons	1 teaspoon soda
1½ cups sugar	2 teaspoons cream of tartar
1 teaspoon vanilla	½ teaspoon salt
6 large egg yolks	½ teaspoon nutmeg
3¼ cups all-purpose flour	1 cup milk

Cream butter, sugar, and vanilla together with hand mixer. Add egg yolks one at a time, beating smooth after each addition. With a wooden spoon, add sifted dry ingredients alternately with milk and beat well—batter will be very thick.

Pour into a well-buttered 8 × 11-inch loaf pan and bake at 350 degrees for about 40 minutes or until a toothpick inserted in the center comes out clean. Cool in pan on a rack and frost with Fudge Frosting. Serves 10.

FUDGE FROSTING

1 square (1 ounce) unsweetened chocolate	½ cup milk
1 cup sugar	2 tablespoons butter
1 tablespoon light corn syrup	1 teaspoon vanilla

Butter the sides of a heavy saucepan and combine all ingredients except vanilla. Bring to a boil on low heat, stirring occasionally, until mixture reaches the soft ball stage. Remove from heat and let cool to very warm. Add vanilla. Stir the mixture continuously with a wooden spoon or spatula until it becomes thick and creamy but still spreadable. If frosting becomes too stiff, add ½ teaspoon light cream and stir until creamy. Frost cake immediately.

HARVESTERS' COFFEE

1 cup medium ground
  coffee
1 crushed eggshell

2 cups cold water
6 cups boiling water

Put coffee, eggshell, and 1 cup cold water in a 10-cup granite coffeepot. Boil for 2 minutes. Add the 6 cups boiling water and simmer for 5 minutes. Remove from heat and add 1 cup cold water to carry down the grounds. Let stand 5 minutes before straining and serving.

3. *A*ll of Her Mother's Children

🍵   🍵   🍵   🍵   🍵   🍵

Envision a spinster homesteader in her midthirties who has owned her own homestead almost a decade, has worked hard, and has doubled her land holdings. She loves the Dakota prairies so much she knows she will never leave them. She also knows she will never marry. She has become the pioneer version of the career woman.

Now envision a blue-eyed bachelor homesteader who comes into her life and changes her mind. She marries him, but she is certain she is too old to have children. He changes her mind about that, too. They have five children in seven years. By then she is going on forty-three, and she is certain she will not have another child. The last baby was a difficult birth, and both she and the doctor predict it will be her last.

She has never had a formal group photograph made of her brood, and when her fifth baby is six months old she tells her husband that now that their family is complete they must have a photo taken of all of them together.

For weeks she sews, making intricately embroidered dresses for the girls and a new suit with a flowing polka-dot tie for the boy. Then the children are dressed in their new clothes and taken to Williston for a beautiful studio photograph. The mother has dozens of copies of the photo made and sends them to all the relatives, near and far.

Two years later, another child is born.

The child is almost grown up before she happens on the photo stored away in an old photo box in the attic. She doesn't need to ask her mother about the photo; it tells the whole story.

Sometime later, though, she does ask her mother whether she really wanted her after having five other children. Her mother replies that the only sadness she felt was knowing that it would be her last child. Then she adds softly that this is the way she felt when all of her babies were born; at her age she thought each one would be the last, and each additional one that came along was an added joy.

The mother never does get another photograph taken of her six children. Things just get away from her. It doesn't bother the last child at all, because she knows she is a loved child. Even today, when she looks at the photograph of her five siblings and thinks of her mother sewing all of those clothes and dressing up "all" of her children for the picture of a lifetime, she can't keep from smiling.

All of my siblings. Clockwise from left: Bernice, Gladys, Florence, Norman, and baby Frances. I came along two years later. From the author's collection.

SØT SUPPE
(Fruit Compote)

One of the loveliest things pioneer women of Scandinavian descent did for each other was to bring the *Søt Suppe*, the sweet soup, when a child was born. It was traditionally brought by the closest friend or neighbor as a token of good fortune meant to restore the mother to good health. *Søt Suppe* was made with any dried fruits available, could consist of only dried apples and raisins, or could include apricots and prunes as well.

1 cup dried apple chunks   ¼ cup whole raisins
1 cup sun-dried apricots   2 tablespoons sugar
1 cup pitted prunes   2½ cups water

Combine all ingredients in a heavy saucepan and bring to a full boil for 1 minute. Turn heat off and let pan sit on stove until cool. Serve immediately in pretty compote dishes or refrigerate for later use. Serves 4 to 6.

FRENCH TOAST

Homesteaders' children who had to walk a mile or two to school on country roads needed a good breakfast, especially when all they had for lunch were cold peanut butter sandwiches, which sometimes froze in the cloakroom. Our mother made us this french toast often on the coldest days.

6 slices bread   1 cup milk
2 large eggs   1 teaspoon sugar

Cut slices of bread that are at least a day old into half. Beat eggs and combine with milk and sugar. Dip bread into egg mixture and fry in liberal amounts of butter or margarine on hot griddle until golden brown, turning several times. Serve with more soft butter and maple or corn syrup if desired.

CUSTARD MERINGUE PIE

Still warm from the oven, this was our favorite pie when we were children. My mother is the only one I ever knew who put meringue on her custard pie. She didn't fuss over it. When the custard was almost set in the oven, she'd beat up the egg whites fast with a fork in a small bowl, add the sugar, slide the pie out of the oven onto the oven door, spoon on the meringue, and push it back in the oven.

For the 9-inch unbaked pie	*2 egg whites*
shell: use recipe for	*½ cup sugar*
Carrine's Flaky Pie Crust	*1¾ cups milk*
(see page 23)	*1 teaspoon vanilla*
For the filling:	*¼ teaspoon nutmeg*
4 large egg yolks	

After making pie shell, refrigerate for 15 minutes. In a medium-size bowl place the egg yolks, egg whites, and sugar and beat for 2 to 3 minutes with electric mixer. Heat the milk to nearly scalding and then stir into the egg mixture along with the vanilla and nutmeg. Pour into shell and bake for 15 minutes at 350 degrees, then lower heat to 325 degrees and bake for another 15 minutes. At the 25-minute mark, start to make the meringue.

Meringue Topping

2 egg whites, at room	*3 tablespoons sugar*
temperature	*½ teaspoon vanilla*

Wash beaters and beat egg whites until foamy; then add sugar and vanilla and beat until they hold stiff peaks. Remove pie from oven and turn heat back up to 350 degrees while you spread the meringue; slide onto center of pie all in one piece with a rubber spatula, then gently seal to the edges. Again lower heat to 325 degrees, put pie back in oven and bake for another 10 to 15 minutes until meringue is golden brown and firm to the touch. Cool on pie rack.

ROCKS
(Oatmeal Raisin Cookies)

These chunky cookies shaped in the form of rocks were a favorite with homesteaders' children. Our mothers didn't often have nuts to put in them, but when they did it was a special treat.

1 cup flour minus 1 tablespoon
½ teaspoon soda
¼ teaspoon salt
½ teaspoon nutmeg
⅛ teaspoon ginger
¾ cup butter or margarine
⅓ cup white sugar
⅓ cup brown sugar
1 large egg

1½ teaspoons vanilla
1¾ cups oatmeal
½ cup whole raisins (plump in boiling water ½ minute, pat dry)
⅓ cup coconut (firmly packed)
¾ cup coarsely chopped walnuts

Sift flour, soda, salt, and spices together and set aside. Blend butter, sugars, egg, and vanilla together with electric mixer until smooth. Add oatmeal and flour mixture with a spoon, then raisins, coconut, and nuts.

On lightly greased cookie sheets drop heaping teaspoons of mixture 2 inches apart. With a floured fork gently firm-up sides and top of cookies to form rocklike shapes. Do not flatten. Preheat oven to 375 degrees. Turn heat down to 325 degrees and wait a minute or two before inserting first batch of cookies. Bake at 325 degrees for 20 minutes until firm in the center and golden brown. Transfer to cooling racks and store in airtight tins. Makes about 3½ dozen.

BREAD PUDDING

Children love bland food, and this pudding was one of our favorites. My mother would make it with the heels of bread she had collected over several days. It was a good way to get milk into us, too, which we seldom drank by itself.

8 to 10 leftover heels and
   crusts of white, rye,
   and wheat bread (a
   combination is best),
   about 4 cups
¼ cup sugar

½ teaspoon nutmeg
1½ teaspoons vanilla
1½ cups milk or enough to
   cover
2 tablespoons butter or
   margarine, cut in pieces

Crumble bread into an 8-inch square casserole dish. Sprinkle on sugar and nutmeg and add vanilla. Cover with milk. Dot butter on top. Bake at 300 degrees for 1 hour. Serve hot with light cream. Serves 4.

4. *L*iver, Black Pudding,
and Antiphlogistine

Why did most of us who were children of Scandinavian homesteaders grow up healthy without the benefit of doctors, antibiotics, vitamin supplements, central heating, refrigeration, and indoor plumbing?

Three good reasons come to mind: liver, black pudding, and Antiphlogistine. The first two we ingested in great quantities twice a year, and the third we had plastered on our chests when the flu season broke out in the dead of winter.

First the liver and black pudding, which Norwegians call *klubb*. According to a vitamin book I have, liver has more vitamins per cubic inch than any other food. My vitamin book has never heard of *klubb*, but if truth were known, it probably exceeds liver. Whenever my father butchered a pig or steer to provide meat for his family, we had them both—back to back. How our red corpuscles must have shot through the ceiling!

In the earliest years before frozen food lockers could be rented in the nearby town with electricity, my father had to butcher in late November and early March. He would cut up the carcass in huge slabs and hang it to freeze from the rafters in his old homestead cabin, which was located a few yards behind our house. The liver had to be used immediately, so we had fried liver *every* day for at least a week, until it was all gone. My mother rolled it in flour, sauteed it in butter, and smothered it in onions. If it was pork liver, she poured boiling water over it first.

Then my mother would make *klubb* from the three or four quarts of blood that my father had saved from the butchering and which had been resting on the back porch, half-frozen, waiting its turn until the liver was used up.

She heated the blood for a few minutes, let it cool to lukewarm, and then added flour until she had a stiff dough. I always shuddered a little when I saw my mother's arms disappear into the bloody dough. She kneaded it thoroughly, then formed round loaves the size of a softball and put three or four pieces of suet into each. The day before, she had sewn small cloth bags from an old flour sack, and in each of these she placed a loaf and sewed up the open ends with a darning needle and strong white thread. She placed the bags in a large kettle of boiling water and boiled them for about an hour, after which she put them out on the back porch to cool. The next day she'd cut open the first bag, take out the loaf and slice it thin and fry it in butter. For the next week we'd eat *klubb* until every loaf was gone.

I wasn't all that fond of *klubb*, and I didn't like liver

much better. But after a month of both of them, I could lick my weight in wildcats!

Now on to the Antiphlogistine. One autumn when the Watkins man made his annual stop at our farm to show us everything in his wondrous suitcase of extracts, patent medicines, and other remedies, he told my mother he had a new product called Antiphlogistine, which she should absolutely spread on the chests of her children at the first sign of a winter cough. He said that he had already sold this miracle poultice to all of the other mothers up the road, and my mother would be found wanting if she didn't buy it. Not an easy touch, my mother nevertheless went for it.

The winter turned out to be an unusually severe one, and in February all of the children in our one-room country school came down with frightening chest colds and hacking coughs. Our mothers, thankful that they were prepared, broke out their large jars of Antiphlogistine.

The instructions said that the poultice must be spread on the child's chest at least half an inch thick and that a warm flannel cloth must be placed over it and tied firmly at the back to keep it in place. So my mother got out her sewing machine and made three flannel cloths with tiebacks. The night she placed the Antiphlogistine on my chest with a putty knife and put the cloth over it, it seemed as though fire went through me, and I became so hot that I ran to a cold corner of the kitchen, sat down in it, and almost fainted. But I rallied, and the next day my sisters Gladys and Fran and I went to school encased from the base of the neck to the waist in a heavy layer of Antiphlogistine. The room smelled so pungent we knew as soon as we arrived that all of the other children were encased in it, too.

We all wore our Antiphlogistine poultices until the start of spring breakup. And spring wasn't the only thing that started to break. After a few weeks of wearing the poultices, the Antiphlogistine started to crack like plaster away from our chests. When my sisters and I and the other neighbor children walked home from school, it was necessary for us to climb through several barbed wire fences. We always lined up and climbed through the fences in one body, and when we bent down, we could hear the Antiphlogistine cracking and crumbling all down the line. It was as if a cement wall were giving way.

When our mothers finally untied the flannel cloths and took the poultices off our chests, we felt as light and frisky as spring colts, as if we could float on air. What's more, our coughs had almost disappeared. Our mothers, watching us play, looked at each other and said, "Thank God for the Watkins man!"

5. A Flair for the Dramatic

☕ ☕ ☕ ☕ ☕ ☕

My sister Barney as a young girl definitely had a flair for the dramatic. Starting at the age of seven, when she set her baby sister Fran down on a hot oven door to warm her up (the baby was wearing long white stockings pinned to her diapers so escaped with nothing more than a hot seat), she loved to do things differently.

The oldest in a farm family of five girls and a boy, she considered it her duty to be the trendsetter, and trendy she was. She followed the changing fashions avidly and was always the first with a flowing cape sleeve, a peplum, or lounging pajamas with two yards in each leg. When she was in high school she acquired a pair of riding breeches along with boots laced to the knees and wore them everywhere, although we had no riding horses on our farm. In a family of coffee drinkers, she favored ornate Ming teapots in which she insisted on serving up green tea for supper. When she became a rural schoolteacher, she exchanged her regular eyeglasses for a pair of pince-nez on the theory that they would make her look older than her nineteen years and would help keep her students in line.

Barney was a luxury-loving Taurus, all right; doing things up nicely and always putting her best foot forward were important to her. So it is understandable that when she inadvertently burned down the privy in the backyard one night, creating a conflagration whose flames shot up into the sky and could be seen for miles around, it was the most humiliating experience of her lifetime.

This is how it happened. Barney was spending the summer at home on the farm with all of us younger children after her first year of teaching, and one day when she was cleaning out the ashes from the bottom of the coal range in the kitchen, she suddenly got the brilliant idea that instead of putting them, as we ordinarily did, in the huge round steel barrel behind the coal shed, she would pour them down into the hole of the outhouse to disinfect the contents. This she did all on her own without telling anyone, thinking that the rest of the family would be pleasantly surprised, sooner or later, at how sweet-smelling the privy had become.

My mother, who was a very light sleeper, awoke in the middle of the night, saw the western windows lit up as with a beautiful sunset, looked out into the backyard, and was amazed to see that the privy was at that very moment going up in flames. She had a hard time waking my father, who was a very heavy sleeper, and when she told him the privy was on fire he didn't believe her and rolled over to go back to sleep. By that time, however, several of us younger children had heard the ruckus, and we rushed downstairs in our nightgowns, crying in unison, "The outhouse is on fire!"

My father sprang out of bed and stared out of the windows. "The outhouse is on fire," he said wonderingly, as if he had been the first to discover it. He pulled on his pants, always at the ready on a chair by his bed, and we all rushed outdoors to view this amazing phenomenon.

As he watched the flames licking toward the brilliant star-studded North Dakota sky, my father said, "Nobody on this place smokes." He did not say it accusingly, nor did he look sternly in the faces of each of his children. Because he knew absolutely, unconditionally, *for a fact*, that no one in his family smoked.

"Now how in the world," he mused, "could this have happened."

At that moment Barney appeared at the back door in her bathrobe, her face as red as the flames, and confessed that she had thrown the hot ashes from the stove into the privy that morning.

My father stared at her dumbfounded. "What do you know! Why would you want to do a thing like that?"

"Deodorize," Barney muttered. "I thought it would deodorize."

My father rubbed his head and shook it.

Then suddenly we saw automobile lights coming from every direction. Our neighbors had seen the flames and, thinking our house was on fire, had jumped into their cars to offer assistance on the scene. Just as they were driving up, my mother's brother, Ole, who lived across the road, came panting up to the house carrying a bucket of water in each hand. When he saw what was on fire, he suddenly dropped his buckets, passed his hand over his face, rolled his rheumy eyes up into his head, and went into one of his horrible laughing fits. He just stood there shaking his head and trying to swallow his convulsions, but he was obviously already out of control.

Meanwhile, the other neighbors had scrambled from their automobiles and were running toward the house, buckets in hand. When they saw what was on fire, they stopped short, their mouths dropped open, and they stood there silently, looking embarrassed. "How . . . how did it happen?" one of them ventured softly.

"Oh, that Bernice," my father said. "She threw the stove ashes in the outhouse. It was a dumb thing to do, I can tell you that."

Luckily, Barney didn't hear this, because she had already retreated into the house and back up the stairs where she sat on her bed weeping hysterically. Luckily, too, that she didn't see the last man who drove wildly up the lane in a pickup truck with a tall ladder hanging out the back. It was George, the perennial bachelor who lived a mile down the road and who had a serious crush on Barney. He had seen the flames and, unlike his neighbors, had taken the time to load a ladder into his truck, thinking that if he could rescue the object of his affections from a second-story window she might look more kindly on him in the future. When George jumped from his pickup, rushed forward, and saw what was afire, he shrugged his shoulders disconsolately. Quickly realizing that it wasn't seemly to look disappointed, he adopted a very sober attitude and lined up with the other men to watch the flames.

There was really nothing anyone could do. My mother debated whether to make coffee and sandwiches but decided the occasion didn't call for it. When the outhouse had at last burned to the ground and the flames had subsided, the neighbors got in their cars and drove very quietly home.

But for Barney that was not the end of it. Although there was nothing left to burn, the next night at midnight, for some odd reason, the fire reactivated itself, and again we were awakened by flames roaring angrily out of the subterranean regions. Interestingly, none of the neighbors—including George—who had shown up the first night came again, but several others who had missed it the first time around came rushing to the scene, and my father had quite a time explaining how Bernice had burned down the outhouse the night before, and now only God knew why the flames had leaped out of the ashes to blaze once more.

For weeks Barney wouldn't go to church or any other community affair. The day my father and my brother rebuilt the outhouse, she remained upstairs with her hands over her ears so she wouldn't have to listen to the pounding. She just sat on her bed and moaned.

After teaching school for many years, Barney joined the U.S. Cadet Nurse Corps during World War II and became a registered nurse. When the war was over she married a Minnesota farmer and took on heavy-duty cooking. But she still did it with flair. When you came to her house for dinner you could always expect something different.

VANILLA TEA COOKIES

While my mother always served strong coffee with her Scandinavian cookies, these dainty vanilla cookies are just what Barney might have served with her green tea.

1½ cups butter or margarine, cut in pieces	2 medium eggs
	2½ teaspoons vanilla
1 cup sugar	2½ plus ⅓ cups flour

Combine cut-up butter, sugar, eggs, and vanilla in a bowl and beat until smooth with electric mixer. Add flour and blend with a spoon.

Flour the hands well and form dough into balls the size of a small walnut and set on ungreased cookie sheets. Dip the bottom of a small (1¾ inch) jelly glass in flour and lightly press the cookies to form rounds of about 1½ inches. Sprinkle lightly with granulated sugar and bake at 325 degrees for 15 minutes or until golden at the edges. Cool on racks and serve with afternoon tea. Makes about 5 dozen.

PEPPERED FISH

Salt liberally on both sides white fish fillets (cod, halibut, perch, scrod, sole, etc.), then marinate in milk at least 30 minutes. Pour off excess milk and discard. Spread soft butter or margarine on both sides before placing on broiler. Grind coarse pepper over fish and broil for 3 to 4 minutes on each side. Serve with slices of lemon.

BARNEY'S SOUR CREAM FUDGE

2 squares (2 ounces) unsweetened chocolate	1 cup coarsely chopped walnuts
2 cups sugar	1 tablespoon butter (to coat platter)
⅔ cup sour cream	
1 teaspoon vanilla	

Break up chocolate squares and melt over boiling water. Pour into a heavy saucepan and add sugar and mix well. While stirring, add sour cream slowly. When mixture begins to boil over medium heat, cover for 2 minutes to decrystallize sugar. Remove cover and keep boiling over low to medium heat, stirring occasionally, until (using a candy thermometer) the mixture is at the soft ball stage.

Heavily butter a large platter and pour mixture onto it. Let cool to warm (not a cool lukewarm). Add vanilla and with a sturdy wooden spoon or spatula begin to vigorously stir the fudge. After several minutes it should begin to thicken, and you can add the nuts. Keep stirring constantly another 3 to 5 minutes until the mixture is thick and creamy and begins to lose its shine. Butter the surface of a large plate and with a stiff spatula quickly transfer the fudge to the fresh plate. Butter the palms and fingertips of the hands and press the fudge into a square about ½ inch thick, kneading the top slightly with the fingertips. Let solidify 15 to 30 minutes and cut into bite-size pieces with a sharp knife. Serve immediately or cover tightly with plastic and save until the next day when it will taste even better! Makes 30 to 40 bite-size pieces.

PEACH SHORTCAKE

2 cups flour
½ teaspoon salt
4 teaspoons baking powder
½ teaspoon cream of tartar
1 tablespoon sugar
½ cup butter or margarine,
  cut in pieces

⅔ cup milk
fruit or berries (for filling)
whipping cream (for
  topping)

Sift all dry ingredients, including sugar, together and put into a large mixing bowl. Cut in butter with a pastry cutter, until mixture resembles coarse meal. Add milk all at once and stir with a pastry fork until dough just follows fork around the bowl. Pat the dough firmly into a buttered 8-inch round cake pan. Bake in a hot oven (425 to 450 degrees) for 15 to 18 minutes or until dough is a lovely golden brown on top. Turn out on rack to cool. While still a little warm, split shortcake in half, lengthwise, and spread between the layers with fresh, sweetened peaches (or raspberries, strawberries, etc.) and top each serving liberally with freshly whipped cream that has been sweetened with a little sugar and vanilla. Serves 6.

PINEAPPLE ICEBOX DESSERT

8-ounce can of crushed
   pineapple
8-ounce box of vanilla
   wafers
1/3 cup sugar
1/4 cup margarine
2 tablespoons vinegar
   (scant)

2 tablespoons pineapple
   juice
3 egg yolks
2/3 cup chopped nuts
whipping cream (for
   topping)

Drain pineapple, reserving 2 tablespoons of the liquid. Line the bottom of an 8-inch square serving dish with vanilla wafers, filling in the spaces with broken wafers.

In a small saucepan combine the sugar, margarine, vinegar, pineapple juice, and egg yolks. Cook over low to medium heat while stirring, until it gently boils and starts to thicken (8 to 10 minutes). Remove pan from heat and place it in an inch or so of cold water in the sink, constantly stirring the mixture until it cools and thickens some more. When mixture is cool add crushed pineapple and nuts and blend. Pour evenly over the vanilla wafers, covering them completely. Cover this mixture with more of the wafers, placing them end to end and again filling in the spaces with broken wafers. Cover tightly and refrigerate several hours. Serve with a topping of freshly whipped cream that has been sweetened with a little sugar and vanilla. Serves 6.

6. *G*lorified Rice

One doesn't ordinarily think of a food fad as hitting a staid Norwegian-American farm community in North Dakota like a rocket from space. My mother and her neighbors were good solid cooks in the Scandinavian tradition, and for the most part they had no time to fuss with cookbooks or recipes; most of their recipes were filed in their heads. But when Glorified Rice descended into their midst, they ran like schoolgirls for their copypaper.

The original takeoff point from which Glorified Rice found its way into our community is murky. It is quite possible that it came from an elegant society tea in Williston, thirty miles distant. Perhaps a city clubwoman invited her country cousin in for a luncheon, and the cousin, having partaken of Glorified Rice in Mecca, couldn't wait to introduce this utopian dish into her own circle. Once there, it spread like prairie fire.

Buoyant in peaks and valleys of whipped cream, it came in many versions: rice with chopped apples and whipped cream, rice with canned pineapple and whipped cream, rice with pineapple and oranges and whipped cream, rice with apples and pineapple and whipped cream, and the ultimate—rice with apples and pineapple and oranges and marshmallows and whipped cream.

No mistake about it, my father and the other men hated it. They invented one excuse after another not to attend Ladies Aid coffee hours, church suppers, covered-dish carry-ins—anywhere they knew they would come up against Glorified Rice.

Who would have thought that such an innocuous confection would subsequently tear apart the very fibers that bound our close-knit community together?

To understand the impact of Glorified Rice, one must understand the climate of the times in the early thirties. We were a couple of years into the Great Depression and the Dust Bowl. Everything was drab, drab. There was scarcely a green blade of grass anywhere. There was no money for luxuries. There was, to be sure, plenty of food. The farmers still had their cows, not so fat as they once were, but still giving enough milk to provide quantities of butter and cream.

Enter Glorified Rice. My mother and the other farm-wives could go to the grocery and buy three pounds of rice for 29¢—boiled up it was enough to feed a multitude. They could add a chopped apple or two, a small can of pineapple, and quantities of whipped cream (which was, after all, free). Heaped up in the gorgeous cut-glass bowls they had inherited from their Scandinavian mothers, it looked like a dish fit for kings.

Their own kings would have none of it. Rice! Every time they walked up to a buffet table and saw the cut-glass bowls lined up in dazzling splendor, shivering with rice-laden whipping cream, they inwardly gagged and turned gray. To a man, they credited their endurance to a steady diet of meat and potatoes, good sturdy homemade bread, and an occasional piece of apple pie. Now—to be faced with this perpetual dish of what they considered nothing but out-and-out mush—it was humiliating.

What it finally came down to was all-out war. Men against women. The battles lines were drawn. Always before, on the third Thursday of every month when the Ladies Aid convened at one of the farm homes, it was traditional for the husbands to bring their wives, go back home to continue their farm work, and return in time for the four o'clock buffet culminating the meeting. The men had always loved to come stomping in—often right out of the fields—with laughter and a quip on their lips for "the womenfolk," as they called their collective wives. They would help themselves to the sandwiches and potato salad, doughnuts and pound cakes, which they washed down with many cups of strong coffee.

Now, thanks to Glorified Rice, those halcyon third Thursdays had gone by the board. One Thursday afternoon when my father dropped my mother off for Ladies Aid, he said, "Last time I had lunch at the Aid something didn't agree with me, so I'm not coming in today. You watch for me around half past four, and come out to the car when you see me."

One by one, the other husbands followed suit. Soon "the womenfolk" were sitting around rather forlornly at their four o'clock buffets while the men sat out in their automobiles revving them up and giving an occasional honk to remind their wives they were still out there waiting.

The women did not give up easily. Would they ever again find a recipe so elegant, so visually appealing, for which they could so easily come up with the ingredients?

It became increasingly evident, however, that the sands of time were running out for Glorified Rice. Even the women no longer lifted the heaping spoonfuls of rice and fruit floating in whipped cream onto their plates with the old exclamations of reverence for the dish's beauty and palatability. The coup de grace was, in fact, just around the corner. And one Thursday afternoon it was struck: the hostess did *not* serve Glorified Rice!

Her husband lurked in the barnyard, lying in wait for the other husbands as they drove in to fetch their wives home from Ladies Aid. He went from automobile to automobile, spreading the word: the war is over. The victorious troops marched into the house with much self-conscious laughter and clearing of throats. As they approached the buffet, they looked warily up and down the table for the telltale cut-glass bowl. It was nowhere in evidence. They wiped their mouths on their sleeves and pitched into the potato salad and sandwich buns.

GLORIFIED RICE
(Rice Fruit Salad)

This was my mother's preferred recipe for Glorified Rice.

2/3 cup rice, boiled until light and fluffy, drained, and rinsed with cold water

15-ounce can mandarin oranges, drained

8-ounce can crushed pineapple, drained

2 1/2 cups miniature marshmallows

1 cup whipping cream

1 tablespoon sugar

3/4 teaspoon vanilla

1/2 cup toasted chopped walnuts (for topping)

In a large glass bowl combine rice, oranges, pineapple, and marshmallows and mix well. In another bowl beat the chilled cream until it holds soft peaks, add the sugar and vanilla, and beat until it holds stiff peaks. Fold into the rice/fruit mixture until it is well covered. Mound-up the salad in a decorative glass bowl and chill several hours or overnight. Before serving, top with the toasted walnuts. Can be placed on individual leaves of gem lettuce to serve, if desired. Serves 6.

7. *O*ne Man's Meat

My father had an all-encompassing rhyme for Norwegian food:

Lutefisk og lefse
Gammel ost og prim
(*Lutefisk* and *lefse*
Old cheese and whey)

For him this couplet took care of just about everything, if you threw in a little *rømmegrøt*, that is. For his day-to-day American-style food, if he could have a small steak and fried potatoes for breakfast, meat and potatoes for noon meal, and a bowl of tomato soup and homemade bread for supper, that was all a man needed for his basic sustenance.

How ironic it was that my mother, an accomplished cook in both the Scandinavian and American traditions, married a man who had little or no interest in food.

Whether it bothered my mother in her early married life I don't know, because by the time I, her sixth child, was old enough to ask her, she had long accepted it as a fact of life and even took a benign point of view.

Even though her husband never complimented her on her cooking, she said, on the other hand he never complained about it either, which was more than you could say for some Norwegian husbands she knew. She would cite a neighboring homesteader who, although his wife was a superb cook, habitually visited his neighbors and stuck around for a meal. Then he would go home to his wife and "brag on" the other woman's cooking. This, my mother said, would have been hard to tolerate. And furthermore, she would conclude, my father often came home with indigestion after carry-in church suppers, indicating that her own cooking was the only food that agreed with him.

Since the Norwegian homesteaders traditionally had *lutefisk* and *lefse* only on holidays, my father chose the other months of the year to satisfy his craving for *gammel ost* and *prim*. He would go to Appam, the small town five miles to the north of our farm, a couple of times a week, and he always stopped at both groceries to buy something. He was obliged to do this, he said, because the two were catty-corner across the street from each other, and the grocers kept strict tabs out the window on every farmer's coming and going. It was the code of the West, it seemed, that you didn't patronize the one and not the other.

He would buy most of his groceries at the first establishment, put them in his truck parked at the wood sidewalk, and then, knowing that the other grocer was watching his every move, he would head directly across the street. This is where my father bought most of his smelly Norwegian cheese. He would come happily home with any form of *gammel ost* or *prim* that the grocer happened to have in his barrel that week. And along with it a large flat box of commercially made *knekkebrød*, a monstrously crisp Norwegian cracker, which was made in twelve-inch rounds. In no time at all the cheese was smelling up the entire kitchen, no matter how many newspapers my mother wrapped it in.

We would hear my father get up in the middle of the night and get out his crackers and cheese and a glass of buttermilk from the pantry. Then he would pull up a chair to the metal cupboard and pull out of it my mother's rolling board to make a little table for himself. I asked my mother once why my father always ate his nighttime snacks at the cupboard instead of sitting at the nearby kitchen table. My mother said that she thought it was because this was the only piece of kitchen furniture he had in his homestead cabin in the five years he was proving up before he and my mother met. Because he didn't have a table, he used the metal rolling board, which pulled out several feet. It was force of habit and what is more took him back to his carefree bachelor days.

Although routinely rejecting any offers of cake or cookies, my father did like a piece of my mother's apple pie; but he ate only the filling and part of the top crust. This suited me to a T, because I sat at his left, and when my father left the table, I always reached over for his plate and finished the golden crimped edge of his pie crust, which to me was the most delicious of all. I was grateful that my sister Gladys, who sat to his right, had already had her fill of pie and didn't fight me for it.

There was only one instance in which my father would eat a piece of candy. Because he went to bed early, my mother and any or all of her children who were still at home would often sit in the kitchen for an hour or two later, talking and laughing, and sometimes we made fudge. After the fudge was poured and cut, one of us children always took the plate to my father's bed, woke him up from a sound sleep, and asked him if he wanted a piece. Without taking his head off the pillow, my father would reach an arm straight out, pick a piece of fudge off the plate, put it in his mouth, and go back to sleep.

Although my father's favorite axiom was "Never monkey around after dark," I recall that once my father came home from the annual board meeting of the Farmers Union Elevator around midnight and woke up all of his six children to have them come downstairs and eat a watermelon he had bought. I remember the incident because it was the first and only time I ever tasted fresh watermelon during my childhood.

Whether he was working in his fields or doing errands in nearby towns, my father came home promptly at twelve noon for his dinner. The one exception to this was when he had been to the coal mine, which took him past John Newman's place. John was a gritty old bachelor who still lived in his original homestead cabin. He wore big black cowboy hats, rode a horse to herd in his cattle, which, unlike most of the other homesteaders, he still raised exclusively instead of ploughing up any of his land for crops.

John also stuck to his old sourdough pancakes instead of going to the store and buying the newfangled bread the grocer was offering. He kept a big black cast-iron kettle hanging on a hook behind his stove, and it was always half full of sourdough. He seldom left his ranch, so his favorite pastime was waylaying any friends from the old days who happened to be driving past.

When his dog warned him of approaching traffic, John, who lived close to the road, ran out and grabbed the horses by their bridles to bring them to a stop. He immediately began to adjust their harnesses, all the while cluck-clucking that they had been put on all wrong. After the harnesses had been realigned to his satisfaction, John insisted that the man come in for a plate or two of sourdough pancakes. He wouldn't take no for an answer; he led the horses onto his ranch and tied them to the hitching post. In later years when the horses had been replaced by trucks, John, upon hearing a motor half a mile away, would go out in the middle of the road and start waving his big black hat.

On those rare occasions when my father was late for a noon meal, my mother would look out of the window and say, "John Newman must have got to him first."

Soon afterward my father would show up, shaking his head, and say, "I can't eat any dinner. Too many of John Newman's pancakes."

Unfortunately, we can't give you a recipe for John Newman's pancakes. If, indeed, he had one, he took it to the grave with him. They must have been good. My father willingly ate dozens and dozens of them over the years without ill effects. He said that whenever the batter in John's cast-iron kettle got low, John would just throw in some more water and flour to replenish it.

What we can give you, however, is my mother's recipe for soda pancakes, which not only my father but legions of threshers and her own children consumed happily over the years.

SODA PANCAKES

When it came to pancakes, my mother was the most opinionated of women. She believed they should be small and thin, and even when she was cooking for a large threshing crew she made them this way. What is more, she thought that the practice of adding eggs and/or baking powder to pancakes was an abomination to civilization, right along with putting sugar in *lefse*, as some of her North Dakota contemporaries were fond of doing.

1½ *cups milk*	1 *teaspoon soda*
½ *cup buttermilk*	1 *teaspoon salt*
¼ *cup butter or margarine,*	2 *tablespoons lard or corn*
cut in pieces	*oil melted with 2*
2 *cups flour*	*tablespoons butter*
2 *teaspoons sugar*	*(for frying pancakes)*

Put milk and buttermilk in a heavy saucepan, heat to very warm but not scalding, and remove from heat. Add the butter, stir the mixture until the butter is melted, and let it cool to lukewarm. Sift the flour into a large bowl along with the sugar, soda, and salt. Add the liquid to it and beat a few strokes until fairly smooth and bubbly.

Heat the griddle over moderate heat until a drop of cold water dances and spits across the surface. It you are using a cast-iron griddle on an electric burner with eight settings, a No. 3 setting is just right for frying pancakes. Drop 3 teaspoons of the lard/butter mixture on the griddle and spread it around with the pancake turner. Drop on the batter with a large spoon, making the pancakes about 3 inches in diameter. Let bake on one side about a minute or until they show dry around the edges and bubbly in the center; then turn and bake on the other side another minute. Pancakes should be a lovely mottled color and very brown and crispy around the edges. Transfer the pancakes as they are cooked to an ovenproof platter and keep them warm in a preheated very slow oven (about 200 degrees). For each batch of pancakes, add an additional 2 teaspoons of the lard/butter mixture to the griddle. Serve pancakes with butter alone or, as Norwegians love them, with sour cream topped with lingonberry preserves. Serves 4.

RØMMEGRØT
(Cream Porridge)

Skeptics who have never eaten this legendary and glorious cream porridge, which Norwegians call their national porridge, are apt to scoff, "How can anything all that good come out of a little milk and flour?" Then they taste it and change their minds. It is definitely a meal in itself and a dish my mother often prepared when relatives dropped in around suppertime and she wanted to serve them something special. Traditionally, nothing accompanies the dish except a tall glass of milk.

2 cups whipping cream
¾ cup all-purpose flour
2¾ cups milk
1½ tablespoons sugar

1½ teaspoons salt
1 teaspoon sugar and
    cinnamon to taste per
    serving (for topping)

Put whipping cream in a large frying pan and bring to a boil for about 5 minutes or until it is reduced to almost half. Sift ¼ cup of the flour over it and continue to cook, stirring constantly, until the cream separates and the butter begins to float on top. Tilt pan and scoop out butter with a spoon or small ladle and reserve it, until you have about ⅓ cup or until all the butter has been removed and a moist curd is all that remains. This will take about 15 minutes of constant cooking, stirring, and tilting the skillet to spoon off the butter. Set the curd aside.

In a heavy saucepan heat the milk until it is hot but not scalded. Sift the remaining ½ cup flour (which has been sifted with the sugar and salt) over the milk and beat vigorously with a round wire whisk until it is smooth. Cook for about 4 minutes, beating constantly with the whisk, until the sauce is thick. Spoon in the curd that had been set aside, beat with the whisk until smooth, and cook 2 minutes more, stirring constantly.

Pour porridge onto deep dinner plates and let stand for a couple minutes to firm up. Sprinkle on sugar and cinnamon. Pour on drawn butter until it makes a golden ring around the porridge. Serves 3.

TOMATO SOUP

3 cups milk
2½ cups tomato juice
1 tablespoon sugar
½ teaspoon dill weed

¼ teaspoon soda
1 teaspoon soft butter per
  bowl of soup

In a heavy saucepan heat milk to very warm but not to scalding. In another saucepan combine tomato juice, sugar, and dill weed and boil gently for 5 minutes to reduce slightly. Remove from heat and add soda immediately. The mixture will foam up; stir it quickly and add instantly to the milk and stir. Pour into four bowls and place 1 teaspoon butter in each bowl. Serve promptly.

The secret of this soup is to keep it from curdling; you must not scald the milk. Add the soda to the hot tomato mixture immediately and then stir quickly into the milk.

Tomato soup is good served with fresh bread and cheese. Serves 4.

SEVER'S APPLE PIE

This is the only pie my father would eat. It is especially good if made with green apples, in which case the sugar should be increased by a couple of tablespoons. Along with thinking that devil's food cake and pancakes should be made only with soda, my mother thought apple pie should have no other spice than nutmeg.

For the 9-inch pie shell
  with lattice top crust: use
  a double recipe of
  Carrine's Flaky Pie Crust
  (see page 23)
For the filling:
4 cups peeled, coarsely
  chopped tart apples

½ *cup sugar*
2 tablespoons flour
½ *teaspoon nutmeg*
2 tablespoons butter, cut in
  pieces

Make pie shell. Mix the peeled, chopped apples with the sugar, flour, and nutmeg and spoon into pie shell. Place the butter around on top. Roll out top crust into an oblong piece slightly longer than the inverted width of the pie pan. With a sharp knife, cut into ½-inch strips. Place over the filling about ½ inch apart to form the lattice top, laying them first one way and then crossing the other way. With any leftover strips, lay around the rim of the pie to seal the lattice strips and crimp with the tines of a fork. Bake at 400 degrees for 10 minutes, then lower heat to 325 degrees and bake for another 30 to 40 minutes until done and crust is golden brown. Brush lattice crust lightly with cream before baking. Serves 8.

8. *A* Born Cook

☕   ☕   ☕   ☕   ☕   ☕

The only one of my mother's five daughters who showed an early predilection for cooking was Florence. From her teen years on she was the one who would help my mother in the kitchen. A typical summer's day of baking on the farm would find my mother and Florence stirring, rolling, and kneading while we three younger girls, Gladys, Fran, and I, would be lined up on the bench behind the kitchen table where we'd be out of the way but could watch. And Barney, with a very martyred look on her face, would be standing at the cookstove washing dishes.

In later years, when both Barney and Florence were married with their own households, Barney became an excellent and innovative cook in her own right, but it never seemed to occur to her in her younger years that she might want to do some cooking on her own instead of being stuck with the dishwashing!

Florence would make these huge puffy doughnuts, then shake them in a paper bag with granulated or powdered sugar and put them in a tin high up on the pantry shelf where we couldn't reach them. Then she'd talk them up— how luscious they were, and she'd dole them out to us one at a time. We'd think we were getting the prize of all time when we got one of her doughnuts.

One summer when whipped cream cakes were the fad she made one so creamy that it scarcely touched the sides of your mouth before it slipped down. She watched my mother make pie crusts, and soon she was making them almost—but not quite—as good as my mother. My mother would always be número uno with the pie crusts.

But bread—that was a different matter. After a certain length of time my mother conceded that Florence could make bread as good or better than her own and handed her the job. Florence had ideal bread-making hands— short, wide, and strong. She always said that she had in- herited our father's blacksmith hands—hands that could throw a sledgehammer over his head and beat a red-hot ploughshare into shape. There was nothing Florence loved better than to plunge her hands into a mass of warm dough. She knew the exact moment when to stop knead- ing, when to punch the dough down, when to make the loaves, and how long to bake.

She developed a three-leaf clover roll recipe that she must have given to hundreds of friends over the years. She gave it to me, too, and I never had any luck with it until I was at her house once when she was making them. The secret, I learned from observation, was to knead each clo- ver thoroughly before placing it in the muffin tin with its two partners.

She baked all of the Scandinavian cookies—some of them that were too time-consuming for my mother. One of these was *berlinerkranser*. Florence walked across the road to see Anna, our Uncle Ole's wife, who had a prized recipe she had brought with her from Norway (see page 126). Anna spoke only in Norwegian, but Florence charmed the recipe out of her—and wrote it down in Norwegian. It became her favorite Christmas cookie down through the years. A combination of hard-boiled and raw egg yolks, powdered sugar, butter, and flour, the dough was hard to work with and had to be rolled in small strips with the palms of the hands, then shaped into wreaths and dipped in beaten egg whites before baking.

One reason Florence was such a successful cook was, of course, that she was constantly talking up her own cooking. Before we even got a chance to taste whatever she made, she'd get the most beatific look on her face, and she'd say, "Wait until you taste this!" In all other ways she was the epitome of modesty. She was very beautiful. She had high cheekbones, a tilted-up nose like my mother's, soft brown eyes, and auburn hair. Young boys and grown men took one look at her and went gaga, but it didn't go to her head. She took her beauty so much for granted that she wore very little makeup and spent no time at all in front of the mirror. She liked pretty, simple clothes and didn't fuss over them. She was a natural hairstylist, and her friends would come to our house with their jars of boiled flax—which was used for setting hair—and she'd put waves in their hair with her strong hands. But her own hair she just washed, put up in a few pin curls, and that was it. She was an accomplished pianist, which she shrugged off.

But her cooking! That was a different matter. "You've never tasted anything like this," she'd say, and even if it was just a piece of cinnamon toast, we'd be convinced.

After I was married and just learning how to cook, I'd suddenly recall one of her recipes I couldn't live without, and I'd write to her in the Twin Cities where she was living with her husband and two young daughters. She'd send it back to me by return mail, written in her strong hand on a pastel recipe card, and at the end, after the instructions, still psyching me up for her cooking, she'd add "These ARE delicious!" or "Voilà!"

In St. Paul, she became known as the bread-baker of her neighborhood. She even had a special coping saw she used to cut her bread—straight from the freezer. The neighbor women would say, "Let's go over and watch Florence saw bread."

FLORENCE'S THREE-LEAF CLOVER ROLLS

1 package active dry yeast   *¼ cup sugar*
   soaked in ¼ cup warm   *1 medium egg, beaten*
   water and 1 teaspoon   *1 tablespoon honey*
   honey   *1 teaspoon salt*
¾ cup boiling water   *3 cups sifted all-purpose*
⅓ cup butter or margarine   *flour plus ½ cup*

Proof yeast in ¼ cup warm water and 1 teaspoon honey until foamy. Heat 1 cup water to boiling in saucepan, take off heat, and add the butter, sugar, egg, honey, and salt. Stir mixture until it is dissolved, then cool to lukewarm.

After the yeast has bubbled up, add the cooled liquid to it and add 3 cups flour. Mix well and let rise 1 hour or until light. Put ½ cup flour on pastry cloth, put dough on it, and knead until the flour is just absorbed. Place in a buttered bowl and refrigerate at least 3 hours or overnight. (Dough will keep up to three days. If storing, punch down once.)

Grease 18 muffin cups heavily with butter. Take dough out of refrigerator and form into three-leaf shapes—kneading each little clover thoroughly before placing in the muffin pan. Brush tops with melted butter and let rolls rise about 90 minutes or until light in the pan. Bake at 375 degrees for 15 minutes until light golden brown. Turn out of pans and serve, still warm. Makes 18 rolls.

POTATO BREAD

This was the bread my mother made in later years when compressed yeast became available and which Florence became so proficient in making.

2¼ cups hot potato water
1 cake compressed yeast or
   2½ teaspoons active dry
   yeast
2 tablespoons plus 1
   teaspoon sugar
1 tablespoon butter

1 tablespoon lard
1 tablespoon salt
7 cups unbleached flour
2 tablespoons softened
   butter (for coating tops
   of bread)

Use potato water that has been drained from a kettle of peeled, boiled potatoes. In ¼ cup of the potato water that has been cooled to lukewarm, crumble the yeast along with 1 teaspoon of the sugar for 15 minutes or until it is foamy. Put butter, lard, salt, and the remaining sugar in a large mixing bowl, add the 2 cups hot potato water, and stir until the butter and lard are melted. Cool to lukewarm. Add 2 cups of the flour and beat vigorously. Add the yeast and beat well. Add an additional 4 cups of flour all at once, stir, and knead the dough just enough to form a rough round ball. Turn the dough out on a wooden board and let it stand, covered with the inverted bowl, for 20 minutes. Knead the dough well, incorporating as much of the remaining 1 cup flour as necessary in the first minute of kneading (do not add any more flour after that) to keep the dough from sticking to board. Knead another 9 or 10 minutes; when dough has been kneaded sufficiently, it will be velvety and slightly tacky to the touch.

Grease a bowl with butter, roll dough around in it, cover with dish towel, and let dough rise in a warm place until doubled in bulk—60 to 90 minutes. (An unheated oven with the light turned on is a good place.) Punch down dough, knead five or six times, return it to the bowl, and let rise again until doubled—about 45 minutes. Punch down, divide the dough in half, and form each half into a ball. Let the balls stand, covered with inverted bowls, for 10 minutes.

Butter heavily the bottoms and halfway up the sides of two loaf pans, 9 × 5 × 3 inches. Roll out each ball of dough into a large rectangle (about 8 × 18 inches) and try to press out any large bubbles with the rolling pin. Beginning with a short side (and using a loaf pan as a guide), roll up the rectangle tightly into a loaf the exact length of the pan, stretching the dough gently as you go along. Seal ends of loaf by pressing in with the fingers and pinching dough at ends. Place loaves seam-side down in pans. Spread each top with 1 tablespoon of the soft butter. Let rise 1 to 2 hours or until center of dough is about 1½ inches above top of pans. Bake in a preheated 425 degree oven for 10 minutes, then reduce heat to 350 degrees and bake for another 35 or 40 minutes or until the bottoms of the pans sound hollow when tapped. Turn out on racks to cool. Makes 2 loaves.

RAISED DOUGHNUTS

1 package active dry yeast
¼ cup warm water
¾ cup milk
⅓ cup butter
¼ cup sugar
1 teaspoon salt

2 medium eggs, beaten
1 teaspoon vanilla
3½ cups sifted flour
granulated or powdered
    sugar (for coating
    doughnuts)

Proof yeast in warm water until foamy. Scald milk, add to it the butter, sugar, and salt, stir until the butter is melted, and cool to lukewarm. Add beaten eggs and vanilla. Place 2 cups of the flour in a mixing bowl, make a well, add yeast and milk mixture, and beat thoroughly. Allow mixture to stand until light. Add 1 cup flour, place on board and knead, with as much of the additional ½ cup flour as needed, until dough is smooth and elastic. Place in buttered bowl, turn once to coat, and cover. Let rise about 45 minutes or until light. Punch down and refrigerate overnight.

Divide dough in half. Roll out each half to ½-inch thickness. Cut with floured doughnut cutter. Place on lightly greased cookie sheets. Let rise until light. Remove doughnuts with spatula and fry, raised-side down first, in several inches of hot oil (375 degrees) for about 1 minute on each side or until brown. Transfer with slotted spoon to wire racks covered with paper towels to drain. When lukewarm, shake in a paper bag with either granulated or powdered sugar. Makes 18 doughnuts and 30 doughnut holes.

WHIPPED CREAM CAKE

This perfectly delightful cake has a unique taste; once eaten, it is not forgotten.

2 cups cake flour	1 teaspoon vanilla
3 teaspoons baking powder	3 egg whites
¼ teaspoon salt	½ cup water
1 cup whipping cream	½ cup finely chopped
1¼ cups sugar	walnuts (for frosting)

Sift flour several times before measuring, then sift together with baking powder and salt and set aside. Whip cream with ¼ cup of the sugar and the vanilla until it holds firm peaks. Wash the beaters and in a separate bowl whip room-temperature egg whites until stiff. Fold them together with the whipped cream. Fold in the remaining 1 cup sugar to the mixture. With a wire whisk fold in the flour in several parts, scraping the sides of the bowl with a rubber spatula to blend all the flour. Add the water last, using a wooden spoon to mix it in and beating a little to blend. Pour batter into two 8-inch cake pans lined with buttered waxed paper and bake at 350 degrees for 25 minutes or until a toothpick inserted in the center comes out dry. Turn out on racks and remove waxed paper. Let cool and frost with Four-Minute Frosting (see page 97) in which ½ cup finely chopped walnuts has been added just before frosting is put on cake.

CHOCOLATE-ALMOND BALLS

In Florence's words, "Wait until you taste these!"

2 ounces semi-sweet
    chocolate (chips can be
    used—measure carefully
    on a food scale)
1 tablespoon milk
1¾ cups flour
½ teaspoon salt
¾ cup butter or margarine

⅓ cup plus 1 tablespoon
    granulated sugar
2 teaspoons vanilla
⅛ teaspoon almond extract
½ cup blanched slivered
    almonds (cut fine)
⅓ cup powdered sugar (for
    coating cookies)

Melt chocolate in milk in top of double boiler until dissolved. Set aside to cool (but not long enough to stiffen). Sift flour and salt together and set aside. With an electric mixer beat butter, granulated sugar, and vanilla and almond extract together. Add chocolate and beat until smooth. Blend in flour with a spoon and add nuts.

To make the dough easier to work with, it can be refrigerated 1 hour. Flour the hands and form dough into balls the size of a small walnut and set on ungreased cookie sheets. With two fingers gently press the cookies firmly to the sheet without flattening. Bake at 350 degrees for 15 minutes on middle rack of oven until cookies are done through but not hard on the bottom. When cookies have cooled to lukewarm, shake in a plastic bag with the powdered sugar. Makes 4 dozen.

ICEBOX COOKIES

⅔ cup shortening
½ cup sugar
1 egg
2 teaspoons vanilla
2 cups flour

1 teaspoon baking powder
½ teaspoon soda
¼ teaspoon salt
½ cup nut meats (cut fine)

In a bowl blend shortening, sugar, egg, and vanilla with an electric mixer. Stir in sifted dry ingredients with a spoon and add nuts.

Flour two sheets of waxed paper and divide cookie dough in half. With floured hands place each half on a sheet of the waxed paper and shape into 7½ × 2 × 1-inch oblong rolls. Wrap closely and chill in refrigerator overnight. When ready to bake, cut in slices ⅛ inch thick and place on lightly greased cookie sheets. Bake at 325 degrees for 15 minutes until very golden brown. Makes 4 dozen.

ROLLED SUGAR COOKIES

The only danger in making these very thin, incredibly crisp cookies is that you may not be able to resist eating a dozen of them yourself before you have finished baking.

3 cups all-purpose flour	3 medium eggs
½ teaspoon cream of tartar	1 cup sugar
½ teaspoon soda	½ teaspoon salt
1 cup butter or margarine	1½ teaspoons vanilla

Sift flour with cream of tartar and soda. With a pastry cutter, combine flour and butter as if you are making pie crust, until the mixture is well blended and crumbly. In a separate bowl beat the 3 eggs well with a wire whisk, then add the sugar, salt, and vanilla and stir with the whisk. Combine the two mixtures and blend very well. Wrap the dough in floured waxed paper and refrigerate overnight.

Take one-fourth of the dough out of the refrigerator at a time, dust with flour, and roll out very thin (to ¹⁄₁₆ inch) on a well-floured pastry cloth. Cut out with your favorite cookie cutters that have been dipped in flour. Transfer cookies to ungreased cookie sheets with a spatula. Sprinkle on granulated sugar or colored sugar crystals before baking. Bake at 325 degrees for 8 to 10 minutes until they are a lovely golden color. Transfer to racks to cool. Makes about 120 cookies if the dough is rolled thin.

PEANUT BUTTER-CHOCOLATE PINWHEELS

Peanut butter sandwiches and peanut butter cookies were staples of our childhood. But Florence's peanut butter pinwheels are a favorite with several members of the third generation.

6 ounces semi-sweet	½ cup white sugar
chocolate chips	1 medium egg
½ cup peanut butter	½ teaspoon vanilla
(chunky is good)	1½ cups all-purpose flour
½ cup butter or margarine	½ teaspoon soda
½ cup light brown sugar	½ teaspoon salt

Melt chocolate over boiling water, then let stand until it is just cool but still very spreadable. In a mixing bowl combine peanut butter, butter, sugars, and egg and beat well with electric mixer. Add vanilla, then 1¼ cups of the flour (which has been sifted with the soda and salt). With a wooden spoon stir in the remaining ¼ cup flour until it is just combined.

Divide dough in half. On a well-floured surface or pastry cloth roll out each half to an approximately 8 × 12-inch rectangle about ⅛ inch thick. Pour half of the chocolate on each, spreading it very thin and almost to the edges. Roll up short side and wrap each in lightly floured waxed paper and let cool in the refrigerator but for no more than 30 minutes. (Do not make more dough then you plan to make cookies. Rolls left in the refrigerator too long will be difficult to slice after the chocolate has become completely hardened.)

When ready to bake, slice rolls gently with a serrated knife into ¼-inch cookies and place on ungreased cookie sheets. Preheat oven to 350 degrees, then lower heat to 325 degrees before inserting the first batch of cookies. Bake 12 to 15 minutes until light golden brown. Remove to racks to cool. Makes 4 dozen.

9. *B*loomers

The Lutheran pastor who served our country church a mile down the road from our farm also served three other country churches in adjoining townships. This not only saved expenses for all the churches but brought the congregations together both spiritually and socially. The pastor was always announcing events from one church to another and urging members to commingle. Summer ice cream socials, held at the various churches, were always a good time to visit the other congregations. These ice cream socials were usually held on the church grounds in the evening, when the ice cream wouldn't melt so fast. A member of the congregation who had an ice house usually contributed the ice, and the other men spent all evening freezing and selling the ice cream (5¢ a cone), with the proceeds used for church repairs and supplies.

Whenever I think of these events, I remember one ice cream social held at the distant East Forks church, which was actually a basement church. Many country churches in the pioneer years were basement churches, initially excavated with the intention of someday having a church built above it but seldom reaching that goal.

I remember this social because it was a milestone in the growing-up process of my only brother, Norman, and his best friend, Lester, who was the son of my mother's cousin Tomas and his wife, Ingeborg, who lived nearby. My mother and Tomas had been childhood playmates back in Minnesota and had later homesteaded on adjoining pieces of land. Their sons were only a week apart in age, Lester having been born at Christmas and Norman at New Year's. The boys celebrated their birthdays together, played together from Year One, talked alike, looked alike, and dressed alike.

At this particular ice cream social, they were about eleven years old and still happily wearing the white knickers their mothers had always made for them.

To learn what happened, we must jump ahead to a week after the event, when Tomas and his family drove in one evening for a visit. While we children chased lightning bugs outdoors and Tomas and my father talked politics in the living room, my mother and Ingeborg went into the kitchen to make coffee. Ingeborg then confided to my mother that something was wrong with Lester. He was morose, wouldn't talk, and had cut his milk drinking and peanut butter and bread consumption in half. She had first thought it was his stomach, but he insisted it wasn't, and in truth a good dosage of castor oil had not helped the problem. Ingeborg asked my mother if she had noticed anything different about Norman's behavior, and my mother said she hadn't. My mother, after all, had six children to Ingeborg's two, and she had scarcely time to notice all of our small emotional swings.

But the next day my mother did ask Norman if he knew what was wrong with Lester. Norman—the original clam-mouth boy—protested so vigorously that he didn't know that my mother knew he knew, but she also knew any amount of pumping wouldn't bring it out of him.

One morning a week later, Tomas and his family again dropped in for a short visit on their way to Williston. Ingeborg took my mother into a quiet corner of the kitchen and whispered triumphantly that, on threat of another dose of castor oil, Lester had broken down and spilled out the entire sordid story.

At the ice cream social, Lester and Norman had been strolling around the basement church grounds, happily ingesting their second ice cream cone of the evening, when they had been suddenly stopped dead in their tracks by three of the Njos boys. The Njos boys were big, burly, bold, broad-faced boys with piercing blue eyes and heads of thick curly hair. They were the image of macho years before macho had been invented.

The Njos boys were not eating ice cream cones. They had their hands jammed deep down into the pockets of their long pants. All Norman and Lester saw were those six formidable legs in long pants planted firmly in front of them, blocking their way.

The Njos boys looked the two smaller boys up and down for many agonizing moments. Then one of them spoke out.

"I see you are still wearing your mothers' *blooo*—mers!"

Ingeborg grew silent just long enough to let the awful words sink into my mother's brain, and then she said in Norwegian, "Think of the humiliation! The situation cannot be tolerated. We are on our way to Williston to buy our boy long pants today, and if you are wise you will take your boy, too."

My mother got the message. By nightfall, both Lester and Norman had their long pants, and neither of them ever wore his knickers again.

HAND-CRANKED ICE CREAM

6 large eggs
1½ cups sugar
1 quart milk

1 quart whipping cream
2 teaspoons vanilla

Place lightly beaten eggs, sugar, and milk in a kettle and let simmer over low heat, stirring constantly with a wooden spatula to keep it just below the boiling point. When it has congealed to the consistency of thin custard, remove the mixture from heat and let cool. Add the whipping cream and vanilla and stir well.

Pour into steel can of 4-quart freezer. Surround with mixture of ice and rock salt. Turn crank slowly until it will no longer turn. Remove ice from top of steel can. Lift off cover and carefully take out dasher, cleaning it off with a spoon as you lift. Replace cover and plug hole in top with small cloth. Repack ice around can until ready to serve. Set freezer in shallow pan to let water drain. Makes 4 quarts.

10. *K*affe Tid

Without their *Kaffe Tid*, their coffee time in midmorning and afternoon to look forward to, the Scandinavian homesteaders would undoubtedly still have persevered, but not so satisfactorily. Whether indoors or out in the field, in good times or bad, they always stopped whatever they were doing and had their *Kaffe Tid*.

It was the job of all the homesteaders' children, from the time they were old enough to carry a tin pail of hot coffee and some sandwiches and doughnuts wrapped up in a dish towel, to take *Kaffe Tid* out to the field to their fathers.

The children watched as they ate, hoping there would be something left for them on the way home. And there usually was. Their mothers always put in a little extra for *stakkars litten*, the poor little ones.

My father taught me to drive when I was fourteen, expressly so I could bring him his *Kaffe Tid* when he was working too far away from home for me to walk.

For *Kaffe Tid* indoors in the early years, most of the homesteaders' wives actually set a complete table both in midmorning and afternoon. The staple, of course, and always present was *smør og brød*, butter and bread. In the morning it was served with jam or jelly. The men loved to spread cold, thick sour cream over a slice of bread, then cover it with rhubarb jam. There were also doughnuts and *fattigman*. *Kaffe Tid* in the afternoon was more substantive. The *smør og brød* were often accompanied by cheese or cold cuts and a cake or cookies together with "sauce," which is what the women called their home-canned peaches, pears, apricots, and rhubarb.

My mother was always uneasy if she didn't have something special in the pantry to serve unexpected visitors for afternoon *Kaffe Tid*. But what really unnerved her was if she had failed to check the butter crock and had run out of butter when company dropped in.

My mother churned her butter once a week in a great wooden barrel churn, which hung on its side several feet from the floor on hinges in a stand. A handle whirled the barrel which shook the cream into butter. Usually it would take less than an hour to turn the cream, but occasionally if the weather was hot and the cream wasn't sour, it might take all day. We children didn't mind churning, but if it took a long time it became boring and we'd begin whirling too vigorously, in which case the barrel might jump out of its hinges and land on the floor, spilling out several gallons of cream. This was about the worst thing that could happen in a farm kitchen, so my mother usually kept an eagle eye on us, admonishing us to "go slow." The best part of churning was suddenly hearing the delicious "plop plop" of great chunks splashing around in the barrel, which meant the cream had given up and turned itself into butter and buttermilk.

If unexpected visitors came early in the afternoon of the day my mother had unexpectedly run out of butter, she'd send Fran and me out to my father's homestead cabin behind the house with a quart of cream in a bowl and an eggbeater. Out of hearing range of the visitors, we'd hand-beat the cream into butter. *Kaffe Tid* without *smør* was a desperate situation.

My mother unfailingly offered coffee to everyone driving into our farm any time of the day, but if it was anywhere near *Kaffe Tid*, they had to have something to eat as well.

DEVIL'S FOOD CAKE
WITH RHUBARB SAUCE

My mother had many of her cake recipes in her head, but she always tested her cake batter before she put it in the pans. She would put a tablespoon of batter on a greased lid from a jar, put it in the oven for a few minutes, then take it out and break the tiny sample in half and examine it with a practiced eye. "Oh, it's too rich," she might say, and she'd add a little more flour. Or, "It's not rich enough," and she'd add one or two tablespoons of whipping cream. She finally got this heavenly devil's food cake down to a science. Her boiled white frosting is also the result of many testings. Put together and served with fresh rhubarb sauce as an accompaniment, they will make any *Kaffe Tid* a festive occasion.

2⅔ cups all-purpose flour　　1½ cups sugar
1½ teaspoons soda　　　　　1½ teaspoons vanilla
½ teaspoon salt　　　　　　3 large eggs, beaten well
3 squares (3 ounces)　　　　1½ cups buttermilk
　unsweetened chocolate　　3 tablespoons whipping
¾ cup butter　　　　　　　　cream

Line the bottoms of three 8-inch round cake pans with buttered waxed paper. Sift flour, soda, and salt together and set aside.

Melt chocolate in top of double boiler and let cool. Cream the butter, sugar, and vanilla together. Add eggs, then chocolate, and beat well. Add alternately the sifted dry ingredients and the buttermilk, beginning and ending with the flour. Beat until the batter is smooth and bubbly. Add the whipping cream and beat a few more strokes. Pour into the three cake pans and bake at 350 degrees for 25 to 30 minutes or until a toothpick inserted in the center comes out dry. Turn out on racks and remove waxed paper immediately. Let cool and frost with Boiled White Frosting and serve with Rhubarb Sauce on the side. For a buffet, this cake is also wonderful baked in a 9 × 13-inch loaf pan. Frost with just half a recipe of frosting and cut in squares or diamond shapes and sprinkle with chopped walnuts.

Rhubarb Sauce

Wash and slice tender stalks of fresh rhubarb in ¼-inch pieces to make 4 cups. (Use about 2 pounds frozen chopped rhubarb.) In a stainless steel pan, combine the rhubarb with 1 cup sugar and ¼ cup water and bring to a gentle boil, then simmer for 10 to 15 minutes, stirring occasionally, until rhubarb is tender. Transfer to a serving bowl and let cool before serving. The sauce will keep, chilled, for about one week. Makes 3 cups.

BOILED WHITE FROSTING

2½ cups sugar
2 tablespoons light corn
 syrup
¾ cup milk
2 tablespoons butter

2 tablespoons light cream
 or half-and-half
 (as needed)
1 teaspoon vanilla

In a heavy saucepan combine the sugar, corn syrup, milk, and butter and cook over low to moderate heat, stirring, until the sugar is dissolved. Bring the mixture to a rolling boil, cover it, and boil rapidly for 1 minute. Uncover it and let it boil, undisturbed, to a very soft ball stage (use a candy thermometer). Remove from heat and beat the mixture with a wooden spoon until it begins to thicken and lose its shine. Have the light cream at the ready as you beat and when the frosting shows signs of becoming too stiff, add the cream, one teaspoon at a time, until the frosting has cooled to lukewarm and is spreadable. Use only as much cream as needed. Add the vanilla. The frosting will look grainy. Arrange one cake layer at a time on the cake plate and, using a metal spatula or long knife, spread a thin layer of frosting over it, add the second layer, then the third. Frost the sides and top using the remaining frosting. Let the cake stand for 1 hour or until the frosting is set.

RÅGBRÖD
(Swedish Rye Bread)

At *Kaffe Tid*, this wonderfully aromatic dark bread, sliced thin and spread with soft butter, is the perfect accompaniment to a cup of strong coffee.

2½ teaspoons active dry
    yeast
1 teaspoon granulated
    sugar
¼ cup light brown sugar
¼ cup dark molasses
1 tablespoon minced
    orange peel
2 teaspoons caraway seeds

1 tablespoon lard or butter
2 teaspoons salt
6½ cups all-purpose flour
2 cups rye flour
1 egg white beaten with
    1 tablespoon water
    (for glaze)

Proof the yeast in ¼ cup of lukewarm water with the 1 teaspoon sugar for 15 minutes or until foamy. In a saucepan
together with 2¾ cups of water, put the brown sugar, molasses, orange peel, and caraway seeds; bring the water to
a boil, and, stirring, boil the mixture rapidly for 4 minutes.
Pour the liquid into a large mixing bowl, add the lard and
salt, and cool to lukewarm.

Add the yeast mixture and 3 cups of the white flour to
the liquid and beat vigorously. Cover the sponge and let
rise in a warm place for 1½ hours. Stir down the sponge,
add the rye flour, and beat until it is well combined. Add 2
more cups of white flour and stir. Turn dough out on
floured board and knead lightly for several minutes, incorporating as much of the remaining 1½ cups white flour as
necessary to keep the dough from sticking to the board.
Knead the dough until it is smooth and elastic.

Put dough in a large buttered bowl, turn it to coat, and
let rise, covered, until doubled in size—2½ to 3 hours—in
a warm place. Butter two 8-inch round cake pans. Punch
down dough, knead it two or three times, and divide it in
half. Shape each half into a round ball, place in cake pans,
and let rise, covered with a dish towel, for 45 minutes to 1
hour or until it is doubled in bulk. Bake loaves in a 325
degree oven for 45 minutes, brush them with the egg white/
water wash, and bake them for another 15 minutes or until

they sound hollow when the bottoms are tapped. Turn loaves out on racks to cool. Makes 2 loaves.

BANANA COOKIES

¾ *cup butter or margarine*
⅞ *cup sugar*
1 *medium egg*
2 *medium bananas,*
   mashed (1 cup)
½ *teaspoon vanilla*
1¾ *cups oatmeal*

1¾ *cups flour*
½ *teaspoon baking soda*
½ *teaspoon salt*
¼ *teaspoon nutmeg*
½ *teaspoon cinnamon*
½ *cup chopped walnuts*

Blend butter, sugar, egg, bananas, and vanilla with electric mixer. Fold in oatmeal with a spoon. Sift dry ingredients together and add to mixture. Add walnuts. In warm weather you may want to refrigerate dough 1 hour.

Lightly grease cookie sheets and drop 1 teaspoon dough for each cookie (cookies needn't be very large). Press very lightly with a floured fork to shape slightly. Preheat oven to 375 degrees and reduce heat to 350 degrees before inserting first batch of cookies. Bake for 15 minutes until firm and very light brown on second high shelf of oven, being careful not to overbrown on the bottom. Makes 4 dozen.

FATTIGMAN
(Poor Man's Cookies)

A Norseman with tongue in cheek must have named these rich cookies so full of good things.

1 large whole egg
4 large egg yolks
1/3 cup granulated sugar
2 teaspoons vanilla
1/4 teaspoon almond extract

1/2 cup whipping cream
2 1/4 cups all-purpose flour
1/2 teaspoon salt
powdered sugar (for
dusting cookies)

Beat together the whole egg and egg yolks with an electric mixer until they are thick and pale, then gradually add sugar, vanilla, and almond extract until mixture is very thick. Fold in the whipping cream, then the flour and salt. Chill the dough overnight, covered, in the bowl.

Dust the dough with flour and roll out half of it very thin (to 1/16 inch) on a well-floured pastry cloth, dusting it with more flour, if necessary, to keep it from sticking to the rolling pin. With a fluted pastry wheel or knife, cut the dough diagonally into 2 1/2-inch-wide strips, then diagonally again into diamond shapes 2 1/2 inches wide. With a sharp knife cut a 1-inch slit lengthwise in the center of each diamond, pull a tip of the diamond gently through the slit, and tuck the end under. Make cookies with the remaining dough in the same manner, rolling out the scraps last.

Deep-fry the cookies in several inches of vegetable oil (365 degrees). Turn only once, frying them up to 1 minute on each side or until they are light golden (lighter than doughnuts). Fry them in small batches and transfer to paper towels to drain. Let cool before dusting them with powdered sugar. Store in airtight tins. Makes about 100 cookies.

11. *G*igi

A child who grows up with four older sisters has only herself to blame if she doesn't get a well-rounded education. My two oldest sisters, Barney and Florence—both of them schoolteachers—actually *were* my teachers. Barney was my teacher in the sixth, seventh, and eighth grades, and Florence taught me in our summer parochial school for several years. Of course they were always correcting my grammar, both at home and in school, which I found irksome at the time, but they told me I'd be grateful in later years. My sister Fran, next up from me, taught me to add and subtract and to be wary of sisters who always win at gin rummy; Gladys, the middle sister, taught me, of all things, how to tap dance.

Gigi, as my father called her (pronounced with a hard g), seemed to grow up without any bones—just ligaments. Even when she was a very little girl she would do somersaults, handsprings, and cartwheels all across the front yard. When she left home to go to high school and she started going to the movies, a new world opened up to her as she watched in awe the country's best tap dancers clicking their way across the screen: Ruby Keeler, Bill Robinson, Eleanor Powell, Buddy Ebsen, Fred Astaire and Ginger Rogers, and Ann Miller.

With the money she earned from baby-sitting, Gladys was able to take a few tap dancing lessons, and from then on, when she came home on weekends, the already unsteady floors of our farmhouse were in peril of falling into the cellar. She did the splits and the backbends. She developed a figure you could die for.

When I was twelve she looked me up and down one day and said ominously, "If you don't do something to shape that up you'll be sorry in a few years."

So she taught me all her dance steps—the time steps and the whole business. With the two of us dancing, the floors bounced so much that my father declared the cellar a danger zone.

By the time World War II came along a few years later, both of us had left off tap dancing. We were both in the Twin Cities; I was trying to finish college, and she was in the secretarial pool at a defense plant that made armored cars. She spent many of her evenings writing to a hometown boy who was overseas in a tank destroyer battalion, and when he came home from the war she married him.

They moved to the Idaho Panhandle, bought a grocery, and had four daughters. With the dozens of varieties of bread she had to choose from in their supermarket, one would have thought making bread would have been furthest from her thoughts. Nevertheless, she began to experiment with sourdough, and soon it became her family's favorite bread. It figures, when you think about it. Anyone living in the Idaho Panhandle should know how to make sourdough.

Her whole wheat sourdough bread (as well as several other recipes that follow) is uncommonly delicious.

GLADYS'S SOURDOUGH WHOLE WHEAT BREAD

For the sourdough starter:	*1 cup water*
1 teaspoon active dry yeast	*1 cup flour*
1 tablespoon sugar	

Mix all ingredients together in a small crock or glass bowl. Cover lightly and let set in a warm place in the kitchen for two days. Stir down several times a day. This will make 2 cups of sourdough starter.

For the bread:	*3 tablespoons softened*
1 package active dry yeast	*butter or margarine*
1½ cups warm water	*2 teaspoons salt*
3 cups whole wheat flour	*2½ to 3 cups unbleached*
1 cup sourdough starter	*flour*
¼ cup dark molasses	*½ teaspoon baking soda*

Measure out 1 cup of the sourdough starter. Put the remaining cup in a 1-pint covered glass dish and place in the refrigerator for future use. (The next time you use it, add 1 cup each of flour and water, let rise, again storing remaining cup in refrigerator.)

In a large mixing bowl soften the yeast in the warm water until foamy. Blend in the whole wheat flour, sourdough starter, molasses, butter, and salt. Combine 1 cup of unbleached flour with the soda, stir into the yeast mixture, and beat well. Add enough of the remaining unbleached flour to make a stiff dough. Knead for 5 to 8 minutes until smooth and elastic. Place dough in a buttered bowl, turn it to coat with butter, and let rise in a warm place until doubled. Punch down and let rise again until doubled. Punch down, divide the dough in half, and form each half into a ball. Roll out each ball into a large rectangle and try to press out any large bubbles with a rolling pin. Using a loaf pan as a guide, begin with a short side and roll up the rectangle tightly into a loaf the exact length of the pan. Seal ends by pressing in with the fingers and pinching dough at ends. Put loaves in bread pans seam-side down and coat tops with soft butter. Let rise 1 to 2 hours until doubled in size. Bake at 375 degrees for 35 to 40 minutes until the bottoms of pans sound hollow when tapped. Turn loaves out on racks to cool. Makes 2 loaves.

SOURDOUGH BISCUITS

1 cup sourdough starter
   (to prepare sourdough
   starter, see page 84)
1 teaspoon active dry yeast
2 tablespoons lukewarm
   water

1 teaspoon sugar
1¼ cups flour
½ teaspoon salt
1 teaspoon baking powder
4 tablespoons butter or
   margarine

Soften yeast in the 2 tablespoons water with the sugar until foamy. Mix with sourdough. Add the salt and baking powder to flour. Cut the butter into the flour with a pastry cutter. Combine the sourdough mixture and flour mixture and knead on board, using ¼ cup of additional flour, if necessary, to make a soft dough. Pat dough to a 1-inch thickness and cut out biscuits with 1½-inch biscuit cutter. Place close together on a lightly greased baking sheet and let rise for 30 minutes if you have the time. Brush the tops with light cream. Bake in a hot oven (400 degrees) for 12 to 15 minutes until golden. Serve immediately. Makes 16 to 20 biscuits.

BANANA BREAD

4 medium bananas
  mashed (2 cups)
½ cup vegetable oil
½ cup light brown sugar
½ cup granulated sugar
3 eggs

1 teaspoon vanilla
2 cups all-purpose flour
1 teaspoon soda
½ teaspoon baking powder
½ teaspoon salt
1 cup chopped walnuts

Combine bananas, oil, sugars, eggs, and vanilla in a large mixing bowl and beat with electric mixer until smooth. Sift dry ingredients together and add, mixing well with a spoon. Add nuts. Pour batter into two approximately 7½ × 3½ × 2½-inch well-buttered loaf pans. Bake at 350 degrees for about 50 minutes or until a toothpick inserted in center comes out dry. (If baking in glass, lower heat to 325 degrees.) Turn out on racks to cool and serve sliced, with plenty of soft butter. Makes 2 loaves.

IDAHO SPICE CAKE

This spice cake is unusually light in both color and texture.

2¼ cups all-purpose flour
1 teaspoon baking powder
¾ teaspoon soda
1 teaspoon salt
¾ teaspoon cinnamon
½ teaspoon nutmeg
¾ cup white sugar
⅔ cup light brown sugar

¾ cup butter or margarine
1 cup milk with
  ½ teaspoon vinegar
  added to it
3 medium eggs
1 teaspoon lemon juice
½ cup chopped walnuts

Sift dry ingredients into a large mixing bowl and add sugars, butter, and ⅔ cup milk. Beat 2 minutes with electric mixer. Add lightly beaten eggs, lemon juice, and remaining milk and beat until smooth. Stir in the nuts with a spoon. Pour into a well-buttered loaf pan (8 × 11 inches) and bake at 350 degrees for 35 minutes or until a toothpick inserted in the center comes out dry. Remove from pan and let cool completely before frosting with Cream Cheese Frosting.

Cream Cheese Frosting

4 ounces cream cheese	⅔ cup powdered sugar
3 tablespoons butter	½ teaspoon vanilla

Let cream cheese and butter soften out of the refrigerator for 30 minutes. Cream together with powdered sugar and vanilla until well mixed and smooth. Spread evenly on cake. If there is cake left over, store in tightly covered cake plate.

12. *E*ntire County

Saved by Rhubarb

My mother could never stand to see anything go to waste—especially food. She preserved everything in her garden. The potatoes and onions went directly on the earth in the root cellar. The carrots were placed in a box of fine sand. The beets and cucumbers were pickled. In the unlikely event there were any surplus peas, my mother canned them, boiling jars for hours in her wash boiler.

And the rhubarb? The rhubarb almost—but not quite—got away from her. My mother's huge rhubarb patch, which was snuggled up protectively against our clump of box elder trees—seemed to feed on itself. Even in the Dust

Bowl years, when either the armyworms or the grasshoppers stripped the garden, her rhubarb patch survived. My brother and sisters and I said, "See? The worms and grasshoppers don't like rhubarb any better than we do!"

My mother would respond darkly, "Just you wait. Someday we might be *thankful* for this rhubarb." And she would bring in washtubs of the red stalks, cut them up and boil them with sugar, seal them in quart jars, and carry the jars to the cellar. There were already dozens of jars of rhubarb from previous years roosting on the wooden shelves down there. She simply pushed these to the back and found room for the fresh ones. After she had run out of jars and storage space, she sent word around to those of our relatives and neighbors who didn't have rhubarb patches, and they would come with their dishpans and washtubs and carry away the rest of the rhubarb. When the patch was stripped, my mother sighed with relief. It was as if she felt, like Joseph in Genesis, that if a *real* famine came along, she had anticipated it and had done her part.

The rhubarb my mother cooked and put in jars she always called "sauce," and it was usually served at supper when we had no other dessert. The "sauce" often went begging, and after several meals of attempted recycling, my mother would surreptitiously put it in the garbage pail that went to feed the pigs. Whether they liked it or not I don't know, inasmuch as it was all mixed up with potato peelings, crusts of bread, and skim milk.

Our aversion to rhubarb, however, didn't extend to *fresh* rhubarb. We loved the pies, turnovers, and upside-down cakes that my mother made with the succulent, tender, fresh red stalks that she pulled out of her patch. Her inimitable devil's food cake served with rhubarb sauce was delectable (see pages 76–78). She often served the cake for supper when the threshers came, and it probably made their day. The pies were superb, especially with a few strawberries mixed in. She made rhubarb jam, flavored with orange, which we also loved. Unfortunately, a kettleful of jam scarcely made a dent in my mother's rhubarb patch and took an enormous quantity of sugar, which was expensive.

Following are some of my mother's best rhubarb recipes.

RHUBARB-STRAWBERRY PIE

For the 9-inch double-crust pie: use a double recipe of Carrine's Flaky Pie Crust (see page 23)
For the filling:
3 cups rhubarb (fresh or frozen—unsweetened)

¾ cup strawberries, sweetened
2½ tablespoons flour
⅔ cup sugar
1 tablespoon butter, cut in pieces

Make the pie shell. Slice or thaw completely rhubarb and strawberries. Toss together with the flour and sugar and spoon into pie shell. Dot with butter. Roll out the top crust the same as the shell. Place on top of filling, leaving 1 inch of crust to overhang the sides. Fold edges of top crust under edges of pie shell and crimp with the tines of a fork. Make five or six small holes in top crust for better ventilation. Bake at 375 degrees for 30 to 40 minutes until done and crust is golden brown. Serves 8.

RHUBARB UPSIDE-DOWN CAKE

1½ cups unsweetened rhubarb (fresh or frozen)
¼ cup brown sugar
⅓ cup softened butter or margarine
½ cup granulated sugar
1 egg yolk

½ teaspoon vanilla
1 cup flour
1 teaspoon baking powder
¼ teaspoon salt
⅓ cup milk
1 egg white

Heavily grease with butter or margarine an 8-inch round layer cake pan. Mix well-chopped rhubarb with brown sugar and spread evenly over the bottom of the pan.

In a bowl cream the butter and granulated sugar together, add the egg yolk and vanilla, and mix well. Add the sifted dry ingredients alternately with milk. Beat egg white to stiff peaks and fold into the mixture last. Evenly spread cake batter over the rhubarb until it is completely covered.

Bake for 30 minutes at 350 degrees on lower shelf of oven. Turn heat off and leave cake in oven another 10 minutes before removing it. With a hot knife or small spatula loosen cake gently from the sides and bottom of the pan before inverting over a cooling rack. Bake as close to serving time as possible. Serve still warm from the oven with plenty of freshly whipped cream sweetened with a little sugar and vanilla. Serves 4 to 6.

RHUBARB JAM

6 cups fresh or frozen   1 large orange
    rhubarb (unsweetened)   5 cups sugar

Wash fresh rhubarb. Do not peel. Cut stalks in half, lengthwise, then slice thin. Coarsely grate orange peel, then cut orange in half and juice. Place rhubarb, orange peel, juice, and sugar in heavy saucepan. Let stand several hours, then bring to a boil for 1 minute, remove from heat, and skim off top. Return to medium heat and cook until thick—about 30 minutes. Seal in hot sterilized glasses. Makes 5 8-ounce glasses.

13. *F*ran's Famous Frozen Peas

When my four sisters and I were growing up together, Fran, who was the closest to me in age, was the least interested of us in learning how to cook. She thought there were other things in life more important than the slavish devotion to the preparation of food. She was our whiz kid, always won at cards, and loved anything mathematical. When I was about to flunk out of algebra my first year in high school, she was so mortified she patiently tutored me night after night. She couldn't bear the thought of a sister of hers never making it out of the ninth grade.

She herself graduated from college in three years, holding down a job in the library all the while. She taught high school math and science for a year or two, and when the war came along she worked in a defense plant, going on to a civil service job in Baltimore. When the war was over she married a navy officer, and they had three daughters who became whiz kids, too, undoubtedly with some tutoring from their mother.

But her interest in cooking remained lukewarm. Quicker was better. Cake mixes were meant to be used, cans were meant to be opened, and the frozen food department in the grocery was her best ally.

Her husband, however, never failed to compliment her on her cooking. No matter how simple the dish she set before him, whether it came from a can or a box or a carry-out store, he always said lavish things about it.

Their three little girls, always bubbling over with schemes of one kind or another, began to anticipate what their father would say at meals, and when he would say it. And then they would giggle. Not their mother's daughters for nothing, they were of an ingenious nature, and one day they secretly rigged up a tape recorder under the dining room table, which one of them could turn on at just the right moment.

At dinner that evening the most exotic thing they were having was a big dish of frozen peas, boiled. At the conclusion of the meal, when their father had finished all of the peas on his plate, he turned to their mother. At that moment, quick as lightning, a small hand reached under the table and flipped a switch. The message was recorded forever for family history: "The peas were delicious, Fran, just delicious!"

FRAN'S FAMOUS FROZEN PEAS

Two boxes frozen peas, any variety. Two cups of water. Combine and boil until tender. Drain. Serve immediately. Serves 6.

14. 𝒜 Man's Worth

I remember one of our ministers saying from the pulpit a long time ago that a man's worth in his lifetime could be computed by the number of times he had been asked to carry pall.

If this is true, my father's life was worth a lot. By the time he died at eighty-three he had carried pall for so many of the men who staked claims to their homesteads at the same time he did that the last thing he would have wanted to do is count.

The early settlers on the Dakota plains formed a bond that neither time nor distance could break. They were all in it together, had come for the same purpose—to build a new life from the prairie grass up. Most of the men who homesteaded in the same township with my father were, like he was, still in their twenties, of Norwegian descent, and still unmarried. In the five years it took my father to prove up his homestead, he came to know and love them all like brothers. He fully expected them to be his neighbors for the rest of his life. But fate intervened.

One of the most difficult decisions my father had to make when he married my mother was to sell his homestead and move his cabin to hers in another township. Here he soon made lasting friends as well, but he never forgot his first comrades, never left off thinking of them as brothers.

A vivid memory I have of my childhood is walking down a street in Williston with my father on our weekly shopping trips. We couldn't walk half a block before he would meet one of his buddies from the early years, and instantly in the middle of the sidewalk there would be old home week. And whether I happened to be five years old or fifteen, the merriment always ended with my father pulling me out from behind his back and saying, "Ya, well, this is the baby!" There would be astonishment at how I had grown, and I would be fussed over.

As the years went by the times became more frequent that someone would drive into our farm and tell my father that yet another one of his pioneering friends had died, and yes, he would have wanted my father to *bære lik,* carry pall.

The automobile had scarcely gone down the lane before my mother began to assuage some of the grief by thinking about what she would bake for the bereaved. If relatives were coming from a distance, the Ladies Aid served dinner after the funeral. The kitchen was in the rear of the church, with only a curtain for a door, and as the minister stood in the pulpit giving the eulogy, the comforting smell of coffee steeping and meatballs simmering on the kerosene burners wafted over the heads of the mourners.

STRAWBERRY ANGEL FOOD CAKE

My mother thought angel food was an appropriate cake to take to the home of a neighbor who had lost a loved one. This strawberry angel food is especially nice.

1¾ cups egg whites
½ cup fresh or frozen
    strawberries (sweetened
    to taste and sliced thin)
1¾ teaspoons cream of
    tartar

¼ teaspoon salt
½ teaspoon vanilla
1⅛ cups sugar
1¼ cups cake flour

Place room-temperature egg whites and thawed strawberries in a very large mixing bowl with slanting edges and vigorously whisk a minute or two until frothy. Sprinkle on cream of tartar and salt and add vanilla. Starting on high speed and moving down to medium with an electric mixer, beat until it begins to form soft peaks. While continuing to beat, very gradually add 1 cup of the sugar in five additions until the mixture is just stiffening. (Do not overbeat.)

Sift together the cake flour and remaining ⅛ cup sugar several times. With a wire whisk, gently but firmly fold in the flour, sifting it out in five or six additions. Using a clean, dry, rubber spatula, carefully pour the batter into a 10-inch tube or springform pan. Bake at 325 degrees for 35 to 45 minutes—depending on your oven—on a center shelf. (Walk softly in the kitchen while the cake is baking!)

When done, remove cake from oven and invert pan over a soda bottle or other narrow-necked bottle (for better ventilation) for 1 hour before removing cake from pan.

Frost with Four-Minute Frosting beaten with a drop or

two of red food coloring to make it strawberry pink. Top with chopped, toasted walnuts and serve with ice cream if desired. Serves 10 to 12.

FOUR-MINUTE FROSTING

This is an easy, lovely, and dependable frosting if directions are followed exactly.

1 large egg white *¼ cup water*
¾ cup sugar *1 teaspoon vanilla*

Put 1 cup of cold water in a heavy 2-quart saucepan. Place egg white, sugar, and ¼ cup water in 1-quart stainless steel bowl with straight sides. Set bowl into water in saucepan and place on high heat. Immediately begin beating with a hand-held electric mixer. When water comes to a boil, turn heat very low, leaving the saucepan on the burner. Continue beating until frosting is thick and begins to lose its gloss. Lift bowl from saucepan, add vanilla (and food coloring, if desired), and continue beating for several minutes. Frost cake immediately with metal spatula or long knife. Makes enough frosting for an angel, sponge, or two-layer cake.

GOLDENROD CAKE

My mother never wasted a single egg yolk; to waste twelve would have been a sin. After she had baked an angel food cake, she must do something with the yolks. This ample sponge cake was a delectable solution.

3 cups cake flour *1½ cups sugar*
2 teaspoons baking powder *1 teaspoon vanilla*
½ teaspoon salt *¼ teaspoon almond extract*
12 egg yolks *1 cup cold water*

Sift flour, baking powder, and salt together several times and set aside. With an electric mixer beat egg yolks in a large bowl for about 5 minutes until they start to thicken. Keep beating and add sugar slowly, then vanilla and almond extract. Add water all at once and beat another 6 or 7 minutes until mixture is thick and light lemon colored. Take a wire whisk and add the flour in five portions, sifting it out a little at a time. Use light, firm strokes to blend the flour but do not beat. Scrape sides of bowl with a rubber spatula to be sure all the flour is blended. Pour batter into a 10-inch tube or springform pan and bake at 325 degrees for 1 hour. Invert cake pan on a rack for 1 hour before removing the cake. Frost with Four-Minute Frosting (see page 97). Top with blanched, toasted almonds and serve with ice cream if desired. Serves 10 to 12.

SCALLOPED POTATOES

When I think back to the covered dishes that my mother carried to funerals, her fragrant scalloped potatoes most often come to mind. Many cooks, she said, make the mistake of putting flour on the potatoes, which isn't needed because the starch in the potatoes will make its own cream sauce in the process of baking.

Fill a casserole dish two-thirds full with thinly sliced, peeled potatoes. Add a sliced onion (red is nice), small or large depending on the size of the casserole. Sprinkle on 1 to 2 teaspoons salt and ½ to 1 teaspoon pepper. Pour on milk to cover (until the level of the milk and that of the potatoes are equal). Dot with 2 or 3 tablespoons of butter or margarine. Bake 1 to 1½ hours at 325 degrees or until top is lightly browned and milk has been absorbed. Stir once in the middle of baking. Do not cover.

15. *T*hree-Day Buns

In today's world of fast food and microwave cooking, it is difficult to comprehend anyone's spending three days making buns for a ladies' luncheon.

The Three-Day-Bun Era began so innocently. One afternoon at Lutheran Ladies Aid the hostess served some uncommonly good buttered buns along with the potato salad, and when my mother and the other women asked how she made them, she said offhandedly, "Oh, these are my three-day buns."

All of the women wanted the recipe, which she passed around, even giving them notepaper to write it down on.

When the women saw how much time the buns actually took to make (three days), they were somewhat staggered but tried not to show it.

The next hostess who had the Ladies Aid also served three-day buns. They may have been just a little lighter than the previous hostess' buns, and after that the gauntlet was down. Each succeeding hostess served a lighter three-day bun than her predecessor, until the buns became so ethereal they were in danger of floating off the plate and sticking to the ceiling like balloons.

The process involved setting a starter dough one day, adding to it and kneading the dough the next day, then punching it down every hour on the hour four times, then shaping the buns on baking sheets and letting them rise all night, then baking them the next morning.

My mother, who was heavily into the competition, ceased all other household operations the days she made three-day buns. The night before she baked them there were four dozen three-day buns rising all over the house.

The Three-Day-Bun Era might have gone on ad infinitum if it hadn't been for a man named Andy. I don't recall ever seeing Andy, but he must have been able to put a wet finger out the back door and know which way the wind was blowing.

One Thursday afternoon at Ladies Aid the hostess served buns, as usual, but they were bigger, browner, sweeter—albeit heavier—than the women's three-day buns, and they were delicious.

"What did you do to your buns?" the other women asked her suspiciously.

"Oh," the hostess answered casually. "I went to Williston and ordered these buns from Andy's Bakery. He has a new sign on the wall that says he will make large quantities of buns for organizations on three days' notice. All you have to do is go in there, order your buns, and pick them up in three days. Andy does all the work."

Except for a couple of die-hards like my mother, who continued to make them for very special occasions only, the Three-Day-Bun Era ended that day. And Andy's Bakery was off on a long and prosperous run.

THREE-DAY BUNS

1 package active dry yeast	⅓ cup sugar
1 tablespoon sugar	1 large egg
2 cups warm water	¼ cup melted butter
6½ cups flour	1 teaspoon salt

On the evening of the first day:
Dissolve the yeast and 1 tablespoon sugar in the water. Add 2½ cups of the flour, beat, and let rise overnight.

On the morning of the second day:
Add ½ cup of the flour, beat again, and let rise 2 hours. Stir down and add the sugar beaten with the egg, the melted butter, salt, and 3 cups of the flour. Mix together and turn out on a floured board. Knead 5 to 8 minutes, using the remaining ½ cup of flour, if necessary, to make a soft but not sticky dough. Let rise 2 hours, turn out on board, and knead a minute or two. Punch down every hour for next four hours. Place dough in a greased bowl, cover, and put in refrigerator overnight.

On the morning of the third day:
Butter heavily two large baking sheets. Take dough from refrigerator, punch down, and cut into sixteen pieces. Shape each piece into a bun, kneading thoroughly in a fold-over action over the fingers. Place 2 inches apart on baking sheets, cover with towel, and let rise until doubled in bulk. Bake at 350 degrees for 25 minutes or until browned. Remove from oven, place buns on wire racks, and immedi-

ately brush tops with end of a cold stick of butter. When cool, slit with a sharp knife and serve with butter alone or sandwich filling of choice.

Note: We adapted this recipe to make it *slightly* easier! Because they had no refrigerators in which to let the dough rest on the second night, my mother and her neighbors had to stay up late to shape the buns, let them rise all night, and get up early on the morning of the third day to bake them.

CARRINE'S POTATO SALAD

Second only to her pie crusts, my mother was known for her potato salad. She always served it when she entertained her Ladies Aid. Alongside her three-day buns, it was robust, piquant, and utterly memorable.

5 cups cubed boiled
   potatoes tossed with 1
   teaspoon salt and ¼
   teaspoon pepper
6 large egg yolks
1 cup cider vinegar
1 tablespoon dry mustard
1½ teaspoons salt
¼ cup sugar
1 tablespoon butter

After sauce has cooled:
2 tablespoons sugar
1¼ cups sour cream
1 teaspoon finely minced
   onion
Before serving add:
⅓ cup light cream or half-
   and-half
For the garnish:
2 hard-boiled eggs, thinly
   sliced
paprika to taste
¼-inch pieces of green
   new-onion tops, if
   desired

Potatoes should be boiled with the skins on, cooled, peeled, and cubed, then add salt and pepper and chill for 1 hour or until cold.

In a heavy saucepan combine egg yolks, vinegar, mustard, salt, and ¼ cup sugar and bring to a boil over medium heat. Then cook, stirring constantly with a flat wooden spatula until mixture is very thick and reduced to more than half (6 to 8 minutes). The mixture will no longer spit and will be dry on bottom of pan—there should be a scant cup remaining. Remove from heat, add the butter, and beat vigorously. Cool to room temperature, add the 2 tablespoons sugar and sour cream, and blend well. Pour the dressing over the chilled potatoes, add the onion, and mix well. Cover and chill in refrigerator overnight.

Just before serving the next day, pour the light cream over the salad and toss up well with a fork. Line the serving bowl with leaf lettuce and spoon potato salad in. Garnish with the hard-boiled eggs, paprika, and new-onion tops. Serves 6.

STAINED-GLASS CAKE
(Red/Yellow/Blue Gelatin Dessert)

Over the years Lutheran women have become famous (many would say notorious) for the never-ending ingenuity of their Jell-O recipes. This refrigerated cake is a little work, but it is well worth the effort for the beautiful finished effect of its stained-glass pattern. It is perfect for the 4th of July or summer church picnic or social.

3-ounce box of cherry
  Jell-O
3-ounce box of lemon
  Jell-O
3-ounce box of berry blue
  Jell-O
3 cups boiling water
1½ cups cold water
½ cup pineapple juice
½ cup pear juice

1 cup water
3-ounce box of pink
  grapefruit Jell-O
2 tablespoons sugar
⅞ cup whipping cream
  beaten with ½ teaspoon
  vanilla and 2 tablespoons
  sugar
1 cup flaked coconut (for
  topping)

In three small bowls dissolve one box each of the cherry, lemon, and berry blue Jell-O with 1 cup boiling water. Add ½ cup cold water to each and let cool. Pour each flavor into an approximately 8-inch square pan and refrigerate until solid. Cut each one into ½-inch squares and run a knife around the edges for easy unmolding.

In a small saucepan combine the pineapple juice, pear juice, and 1 cup water and bring to a full rolling boil. Pour over the pink grapefruit Jell-O and 2 tablespoons sugar and stir until dissolved. Let cool completely and refrigerate until the mixture is thickened but still pourable or about 25 to 30 minutes. Whip cream until stiff and fold together with the grapefruit Jell-O mixture. Unmold the Jell-O squares and combine well in a large bowl. Then fold the whipped cream/grapefruit Jell-O mixture over the squares until it is well blended. Pour into an 8-inch tube pan and chill until very firm. An hour before serving, set tube pan in warm water for several seconds and loosen the sides of the cake with a warm knife. Invert the pan over a large decorative plate. Sprinkle the coconut lightly enough over the sides, top, and center of cake to still let the mosaic pattern of the cake show through. Keep refrigerated until ready to serve. Serves 12.

16. The Nine Days of Christmas

When today's children think of Christmas, they think of gifts. When I was a child I thought of food and celebrations. Gifts were the least part of my childhood Christmases. But the celebrations! That was a different matter.

The active festivities get into full swing in the midafternoon of Christmas Eve when my father brings in the tree and sets it up in the front room. Norwegian tradition holds that the tree must not be decorated until Christmas Eve. My mother is still in the kitchen baking the last piece of Christmas *lefse* on the top of her cast-iron cookstove—a task she has been at since morning. In a few minutes the pungent scent of damp pine mingles with the aroma of fresh *lefse*, and we know that Christmas week has started in earnest.

The box of decorations has already been brought down from the attic. My four sisters and my brother and I dive into the box and begin hanging things on the tree. Because my father—who believed that if you've seen one pine tree you've seen them all—had grabbed the first tree at hand leaning against the hardware store in town a month earlier, our tree is never a very pretty tree. This doesn't matter to us. The important thing is that it *smells* like a Christmas tree.

My older sisters drape the red and green garlands artistically around the branches. My brother gets up on a chair and tries to get the snow angel, already battered from previous years' attempts, to sit straight on the top branch. Then we all reach for our favorite ornaments and try to hang them on choice spots before someone else gets there. Arguments ensue. My mother sticks her head in from the kitchen and says she doesn't want any quarreling on Christmas Eve. We simmer down and work quietly. The tree begins to take on an aura, and we are awed. We feel the Christmas spirit descending on us.

It is now four o'clock, and in my memory of these childhood Christmas Eves it always starts to snow at this time. An eerily quiet snow, as if the North Dakota wind knows it is not supposed to blow on Christmas Eve. I know that there must have been a few Christmas Eves in my childhood when it didn't snow and the wind blew instead, but I don't remember these; they have been erased from my memory.

The creaky old candleholders are the last to go on the tree. The candles will be lit for only a few minutes before we pass out the gifts later in the evening.

My older sisters now go into the kitchen to help my

mother complete preparations for our festive supper. My brother, Norman, opens up the cellar hatch in the pantry, descends into the nether regions, and brings up the (oh, joy) ice cream freezer, which has been stored down there since last Christmas. He sets it on a thick throw rug in the corner of the kitchen. My mother pours the "makings," the mixture of eggs, cream, sugar, and vanilla she has stirred up earlier in the day, into the steel freezer can and sets it in the wooden shell of the freezer. My father brings the gunnysack filled with the ice he has chopped out of the stock tank at the windmill.

Norman packs ice and salt around the can and starts to turn the handle. We three little girls protest. We know that we get to turn it until the handle goes hard. We take turns sitting on the floor and turning the handle until it offers resistance; then Norman takes over. When the handle will no longer budge, Norman unpacks just enough of the ice and salt so that the cover of the container may be removed and we can see the actual ice cream. We have our teaspoons in hand, knowing that each of us gets to dip out just one spoonful before the cover goes back on and the freezer goes out on the back porch until supper. As we taste, the icy scent of the vanilla cream going up our nostrils mingles with the smell of freshly baked *lefse*, meatballs frying on the stove, and the aromatic scent of pine, and we know that Christmas is imminent.

Activity in the kitchen is becoming more frenzied. Barney has placed the extra leaf in the table, spread a white linen tablecloth, and is setting around the good dishes and silverware. My mother is putting the *lutefisk* in a large pan of boiling water, and Florence is mashing potatoes. My father is generating the mantles on the big gas lamp preparatory to hanging it on a hook in the ceiling over the festive supper table.

Dusk is falling outside, and it is still snowing as we look out of the south window and see our Uncle Ole and his wife, Anna, walking across the road. They always take Christmas Eve supper with us. Ole is helping Anna, who has a short leg, through the two barbed-wire fences they must climb to get from their farm to ours. My father turns up the gas lamp and hangs it. The beautiful incandescent light, so different from the kerosene lamps we use on ordinary days, floods the kitchen.

Now we are gathered around the table, ten strong, the snow still falling behind the windows. My mother and father, Ole and Anna, my brother, my four sisters, and me. The piano bench has been brought in for two of us smaller girls to sit on, because there are not ten chairs in the house. My mother brings the *lutefisk* glistening with butter on a platter, my older sisters serve the meatballs in gravy, the mashed potatoes, and a casserole of macaroni and tomatoes. The *lefse* is already on the table, buttered and rolled up in serving portions on a huge platter.

By the time we are ready for dessert, the windows are so dark we can no longer see the falling snow, and the gas lamp above us seems to burn brighter. When my older sisters start to clear the table, my father says, "I suppose you kids didn't leave any room for ice cream. I guess Ole and I are going to have to eat it all." Ole thinks this is hilarious and starts one of his giddy laughs he can't stop. Anna purses her lips and looks sideways at him. He straightens up.

Norman leaves the table, goes out to the porch, and brings in the ice cream freezer and sets it beside my mother's place. He has scraped the ice off the top and taken the cover off. My sisters bring the saucers, and my mother dishes up the ice cream with a long-handled spoon. It is too delicious for words. We eat silently. The saucers are passed back for seconds. My brother has thirds. After all, he says, he did all the work.

As soon as we leave the table, my father, Norman, and

Ole go out to the barn to milk the cows. My father says that Ole doesn't have to go because he has already milked his own cows, but Ole wants to go anyway.

My mother settles Anna down in a chair by the stove. My mother washes, my older sisters and Anna dry, and we three little girls run back and forth to cupboard and pantry putting the dishes away. Then we get out bowls and fill them with unshelled nuts, apples, hard Christmas candy, and Christmas cookies. We bring them into the front room and set them near the tree. The men come in with their pails of milk, and they pour the milk in the cream separator in the pantry. Norman cranks up the handle, and for a few minutes the loud hum of the separator vibrates through the house.

The men wash their hands at the dry sink and join the rest of us in the front room. It is time for the tree lighting and the gifts. We three little girls giggle and fidget and skip excitedly around the tree.

My mother and Anna go into the bedroom and come back with their gifts wrapped in plain brown paper. They put them under the tree. Then my father goes back out to the kitchen and comes back with a pail of water he has pumped from the cistern and sets it beside the tree as a precaution against fire. Norman carefully lights with kitchen matches the dozen candles in their metal candleholders on the tree. They glow brilliantly for a few minutes while my father sits at the ready with his pail of water. He tells Norman to blow out the candles, and then we little girls are allowed to pass out the gifts.

Everyone gets a gift. We girls get clothes—mittens, stocking caps, scarves, nightgowns. Norman and my father and Ole get neckties. My mother has made Anna an apron, and Anna has crocheted doilies for my mother.

After the gifts have been admired, we sit around cracking nuts and eating apples, candy, and cookies until almost midnight. Then Ole and Anna light their lantern they have brought with them. It has stopped snowing, and they walk home across the moonlit snow. We watch through the window until the lantern disappears into their house across the road and reappears in their window.

We are invited to spend Christmas Day with my mother's cousin Tomas and his family, who live a mile down the road. My mother and Tomas grew up together in Minnesota, met again in North Dakota, and homesteaded on adjoining land. After proving up his homestead, Tomas went back to Minnesota, married his betrothed, and brought her back to his homestead. He and Ingeborg have two children, Lester, who is my brother's age, and Myrtle, who is a year older than I am. Ingeborg delivered my mother's first two children at a time when there was not a midwife to be found on the prairie. She and my mother are closer than sisters.

An ample woman with a rollicking laugh, Ingeborg is a bounteous cook. She has a round table which she can expand to fill up her entire kitchen. Tomas, an expert carpenter, built their house, which is huge by pioneer standards. It has three bedrooms up and one bedroom down. But the most fantastic room in the house is the pantry. It is a large walk-in closet with floor-to-ceiling shelves on two sides and in the center a built-in worktable with a rolling board. My mother always says that the reason Ingeborg has such a neat kitchen is that she does all her work in the pantry where it doesn't show.

By the time we arrive for Christmas dinner, the table is set for twelve people; it is loaded, and it is beautiful. Ingeborg has lovely Scandinavian china and antique water glasses of red and gold. In addition to *lutefisk*, *lefse*, and mashed potatoes, she serves roast pork and rich brown gravy. Lining the table are watermelon pickles, raisin breads, preserves, and jellies. For dessert there is pumpkin pie with whipped cream.

Even after my siblings and I were grown up, some of us managed to get home in the early 1940s to spend Christmas Day at Ingeborg's house. Clockwise from left: Lester Quie, Ingeborg, myself, my mother, my sisters Barney and Fran, and Myrtle Quie. My father had gone home to milk the cows, and Tomas was recruited to take the picture. From the author's collection.

After dinner Tomas and my father sit in the living room and smoke cigars while the women and all of us girls wash and dry the dishes. Then Ingeborg and my mother and my oldest sisters settle around the cleared table to talk, and Myrtle takes Gladys and Fran and me upstairs to play. My sisters and I are awed that Myrtle has her very own bedroom. Across the hall is the spare bedroom, which is rented out to the schoolteacher. Far down the back corridor is Lester's bedroom, a cunning hideout for a boy, because one must go three steps back down to reach it. Lester and Norman are already there, playing Lester's gramophone with the cylindrical records. "Jingle Bells" is blaring out.

Myrtle's room is neat as a pin. She even has a dressing table. Her doll is on the bed, a bald-headed doll with two faces. One face is laughing, and when the neck is turned the other face is crying. Myrtle is not overly fond of the doll and sometimes grimaces when she looks at it, but it is her only doll so she puts up with it. We aren't interested in playing with dolls anyway. What we really want to do is play cards—old maid and gin rummy—and Uncle Wiggily. Myrtle gets out the cards, and we settle in a ring on the bed. We tire of old maid fast, and Fran, who is the card-shark in the group, wins all the gin rummy hands. There is a short brouhaha when the rest of us accuse her of cheating, which she denies. Myrtle gets out the Uncle Wiggily board; it's harder to cheat at Uncle Wiggily, and besides, it's our favorite game. We spend the next couple of hours drawing the yellow and red cards, reading them out loud, and trying to get our buttons past the way stations on the board.

At four o'clock Ingeborg calls up the stairway, "Myrrr-tle?" which is the signal for Myrtle to go down and set her Christmas cookies out for *Kaffe Tid*. We all troop down to the kitchen. Myrtle is a fantastic cookie maker. Her *sandbakkels* are incredible—each one a perfect fluted cup of flaky pastry. We can't make *sandbakkels* at our house because we don't have the baking tins. Myrtle passes her cookies around to the grown-ups who are having their coffee around the kitchen table. We take our own cookies back upstairs, because we have got to get back to that Uncle Wiggily game. We are rabid for Uncle Wiggily, and none of us has won yet.

It seems that we haven't even started to play before Ingeborg again calls, "Myrrrtle?" and it's time for her to go back down to the kitchen to help her mother get supper. My father and Norman have already driven home to milk the cows.

An hour later we are all sitting around the supper table again, having potato salad and a platter of *speke kjøtt* (dried beef), sliced thick, which Ingeborg herself has cured in the smokehouse. My father says he can make a meal of

Ingeborg's *speke kjøtt* alone. Preserves, pickles, and Christmas breads again line the table. For dessert Myrtle brings out of the pantry a frosted spice cake which she has made herself. Left to her own devices in the pantry, Myrtle is a veritable child prodigy.

Again we all pitch in to help wash the dishes, and then we little girls head back upstairs to finish that Uncle Wiggily game. No one has got Uncle Wiggily directly over to Dr. Possum's house yet without having to start over, and the race is beginning to resemble the last laps of the Indianapolis 500. We can hear the grown-ups laughing and talking around the kitchen table as they have a final cup of coffee. Norman and Lester are playing the gramophone again. This time it's "Lady of Spain."

My mother calls up the stairs, "Girrrls? Time to go home." We resignedly fold up the board and make Myrtle promise that she will bring it to our house when they come on New Year's Day.

Every day throughout the remainder of Christmas week we either entertain relatives and friends at our house or we go to theirs. Either way it is a noon-to-midnight celebration.

And every night, whether we are at home or elsewhere, there is the delicious anticipation of being invaded by *julebukkers*. Freely translated, *julebukkers* are Norwegian Christmas fools. But why would people want to make fools of themselves at Christmas? At Halloween, perhaps. But at Christmas? A question no true Norwegian asks or answers. They just enjoy. Not actually enjoy the *julebukkers* themselves as much as the foretaste of their appearance, because as the years pass, they appear less and less often.

Here is how *julebukking* works. Some night during Christmas week, several children between the ages of twelve and twenty-five in a farm family will suddenly come up with the idea, all on their own, to go Christmas fooling, if they can recruit a dozen or so other young people in neighboring families. They ransack their mother's ragbag and attic and dig out tattered trousers, old coonskin coats from bygone days, and torn white stockings or grocery sacks they can cut up for masks.

As darkness descends on the prairie, they requisition the family automobile and, dressed in their rags, they go to the next farm to enlist more recruits as they shout, "Come on! We're going Christmas fooling!"

Caught up in the spontaneous derring-do, the young people on this farm instantly commandeer *their* mother's ragbag and join the brigade. After at least a dozen troops have answered the call, the fun begins. From then until midnight they drive wildly from farm to farm, not only in their own township but in contiguous townships. They pound on doors, which are thrown open in welcome by the incredulous occupants who have been waiting, night after night, for the legendary *julebukkers* who seldom materialize. The Christmas foolers dance through the house, making fools of themselves, but always silent as ghosts, while the members of the household throw out loud guesses as to their identity. Then as suddenly as they came, the *julebukkers* run out the door, jump in their cars, and go to the next farm. At midnight, after having driven through the countryside spreading delight and renewed faith in a myth that is fading, the *julebukkers* end up at the farm of the original instigators. There they unmask and ingest cup after cup of hot cocoa and Christmas cookies as they relive the night's performance, always boasting that not once was their cover broken.

So Christmas week is coming to an end, and New Year's Eve is upon us. It is a quiet reflection of Christmas Eve. For my mother and father, although they never mention it, this is a special day; they were married on New Year's Eve. We again have a festive supper. The candles on the tree are lit for a second time and allowed to burn almost down to their holders as my father sits sentinel with his pail of water.

On New Year's Day Tomas and his family come, and they stay from noon until midnight. Myrtle, true to her promise, has brought her Uncle Wiggily game, which, alternately with eating, we play all day long. When we hear my father and Tomas turn the radio on for the eleven o'clock news, which is the final ritual of our nine days of Christmas, we little girls know that there is no way one of us is going to land Uncle Wiggily squarely into Dr. Possum's house in the time left to us. We have been delayed too many times by the Skillery Skallery Alligator and the Bad Pipsisewah. We fold up the board and Myrtle says, "We'll finish this game next Christmas at my house."

NORWEGIAN MEATBALLS

No Norwegian Christmas Eve dinner would be complete without meatballs served with mashed potatoes and *lefse* as accompaniments.

½ pound lean ground beef	*For the gravy:*
½ pound lean ground pork	*3 tablespoons drippings*
1 egg, beaten lightly	*and/or butter*
1 tablespoon light cream or	*¼ cup flour*
half-and-half	*2 cups water*
1½ teaspoons sugar	*1½ teaspoons salt*
1½ teaspoons salt	*pepper to taste*
¼ teaspoon pepper	*1 teaspoon sugar*
½ teaspoon nutmeg	

In a mixing bowl place all ingredients for meatballs and mix thoroughly together. Flour the hands to keep them from sticking and form tablespoons of the mixture into balls (large walnut sized). Let balls dry on cutting board until all have been made.

Put 1 tablespoon of butter in heavy frying pan, melt to sizzling, and put in meatballs. Cook slowly over moderately low heat, shaking the pan to brown evenly on all sides, until meatballs are cooked through on the inside (20 to 30 minutes). They should be very brown and crusty. Remove meatballs to a warm dish with slotted spoon.

Pour off drippings from pan, leaving the brown crusty particles. Measure 3 tablespoons drippings, or add enough butter to measure a total of 3 tablespoons fat, and return to pan. Add the ¼ cup flour and with a fork brown it in the drippings over medium heat, scraping up the brown bits clinging to the sides and bottom of the pan, for 2 minutes. Add 2 cups of water in a stream and, stirring constantly, bring the sauce to a boil, then simmer for 3 minutes until gravy is very smooth. Stir in 1½ teaspoons salt, pepper to taste, and 1 teaspoon sugar. Add the meatballs and simmer for several minutes, stirring occasionally, until the meatballs are heated through. Transfer meatballs and gravy to a heated tureen and serve, along with a bowl of mashed potatoes topped with melted butter and paprika. Serves 4.

SCANDINAVIAN CINNAMON RAISIN BREAD
(julekake)

¾ cup raisins
¾ cup milk
½ cup sugar plus 1
    teaspoon
¼ cup butter, cut in pieces
1 teaspoon salt
2½ teaspoons active dry
    yeast

¼ cup water
1 large egg, beaten lightly
4½ cups all-purpose flour
2 teaspoons cinnamon
1 tablespoon softened
    butter

Drop raisins in boiling water ½ minute to plump. Drain, pat dry, and chop. Scald milk and pour over ¼ cup of the sugar, the ¼ cup butter, and salt in a large mixing bowl. Stir until butter is melted and cool to lukewarm. Proof yeast with 1 teaspoon of the sugar in ¼ cup lukewarm water until foamy.

Combine yeast and egg with milk liquid in bowl. Add 2 cups of the flour and beat well. Add third cup of flour, then turn dough out on board and knead with the fourth cup, using an additional ½ cup or more, if necessary, to keep dough from sticking to the board. Knead dough lightly for several minutes until it is smooth and elastic, form into a ball, and place in a buttered bowl. Cover with a dish towel and let rise until doubled. Punch down, turn it to coat with butter in the bowl, and let rise again until doubled in bulk—about an hour—in a warm place.

Butter the bottom and halfway up the sides of one loaf pan, 9 × 5 × 3 inches. Punch down dough, knead it two or three times, and roll out on an unfloured surface into a 14 × 8-inch rectangle, pressing out any large bubbles with the rolling pin. Combine the remaining ¼ cup sugar with the cinnamon and sprinkle evenly on dough, then sprinkle on raisins. Beginning with a short side, roll up dough tightly and pinch ends together to seal. Arrange the loaf seam-side down in loaf pan. Spread top with softened butter. Cover and let rise until the center of the loaf has risen 1½ inches above the top of pan. Bake at 350 degrees for 45 minutes or until brown. Turn out on rack to cool. Makes 1 loaf.

SCALLOPED MACARONI
AND TOMATOES

My mother and her neighbors often served macaroni dishes and potatoes in the same meal, which seems strange, but no stranger than serving *lefse* and mashed potatoes together, which was de rigueur!

7-ounce box of elbow macaroni	2 tablespoons sugar
28-ounce can of whole tomatoes, cut up	1 cup crushed soda crackers
2 tablespoons minced onion	2 tablespoons margarine, cut in pieces

Parboil macaroni and drain before placing in a 1½-quart casserole dish. Add tomatoes, onion, and sugar and stir around a little. Spread crackers evenly around on top. Dot with margarine. Bake at 350 degrees for 30 minutes. Serves 4.

GINGER CARROTS

6 or 8 large carrots, scraped and sliced to ½ inch	1 teaspoon honey
	1 teaspoon salt
	pepper to taste
½ teaspoon ginger	2 tablespoons butter or margarine, cut in pieces
1 teaspoon lemon juice	

Place carrots in a medium-size baking dish. Cover with remaining ingredients and dot with butter. Cover the dish and bake in a 350 degree oven for 30 to 40 minutes or until carrots are tender. Serves 6.

HASSEL NÖT TÅRTA
(Hazelnut Meringue Torte)

In my book *Nothing to Do but Stay*, I tell of eating this divine dessert (as well as the three recipes that follow) at the home of our Swedish friends, the Lundstroms, during the Thanksgiving holidays.

½ cup butter or margarine
½ cup sugar
4 egg yolks
1 teaspoon vanilla
⅓ cup milk
1 cup all-purpose flour
1 teaspoon baking powder
½ teaspoon salt

For the meringue:
4 egg whites
¼ teaspoon cream of tartar
pinch of salt
½ teaspoon vanilla
¾ cup sugar
½ cup hazelnuts, skinned, toasted, and chopped

In a bowl with an electric mixer cream butter and ½ cup sugar together, then add egg yolks, one at a time, and 1 teaspoon vanilla. Stir in the milk and the flour (which has been sifted with the baking powder and salt) and blend the batter until it is smooth. Spread it in a well-buttered 9-inch square baking pan.

Wash the beaters and in a separate bowl beat the room-temperature egg whites with the cream of tartar and a pinch of salt until they hold soft peaks. Add the ½ teaspoon vanilla and ¾ cup sugar, a little at a time, until the meringue holds stiff peaks. Fold in the chopped hazelnuts (pecans or walnuts may be used in the meringue if desired). Spread meringue evenly over the batter and bake in a slow oven (300 degrees) for 1 hour. Cool in pan on a rack. To serve, cut in squares and top with soft chocolate ice cream or Chocolate Whipped Cream. Serves 9.

Chocolate Whipped Cream

1 cup whipping cream
1 tablespoon cocoa

3 tablespoons sugar
1 teaspoon vanilla

Combine all ingredients in a small bowl and chill for 1 hour. Beat mixture until stiff when ready to serve.

SCALLOPED CORN CASSEROLE

1-pound can cream-style
corn
1-pound can whole kernel
corn (drained)
¼ cup minced onion
¾ cup milk
½ cup light cream or half-
and-half

⅛ teaspoon pepper
2 cups crushed soda
crackers
2 tablespoons butter, cut in
pieces

In a mixing bowl combine all ingredients except butter and spoon the mixture into a buttered 1½-quart shallow baking dish. Dot with butter. Bake in a 325 degree oven for 30 minutes, then stir the mixture and reduce heat to 300 degrees and bake for another 30 minutes. Serves 4 to 6.

APPLE SALAD

3 cups chilled whipping
cream
⅓ cup sugar
2 teaspoons vanilla
8 cups coarsely chopped
peeled apples

16 large marshmallows,
halved
1 cup well-drained
pineapple tidbits
1 cup blanched whole
almonds, toasted and
chopped fine

In a chilled bowl whip the cream until it holds soft peaks. Add the sugar and vanilla while beating continuously, until the cream holds stiff peaks. Fold in the apples, marshmallows, and pineapple. Mound-up in a clear glass serving bowl. Garnish with almonds. Keep well chilled until serving. Serves 8 to 10.

TOMATO ASPIC CROWN

This dish can make a beautiful centerpiece for the holiday table.

2 tablespoons unflavored gelatin	1 tablespoon minced onion
½ cup cold water	½ teaspoon celery seeds
4 cups tomato juice	3 whole cloves
4 teaspoons sugar	½ teaspoon salt
	2 teaspoons lemon juice

Sprinkle gelatin over the cold water and let soften for 15 minutes. In a heavy saucepan, combine the tomato juice, sugar, minced onion, celery seeds, whole cloves, and salt; bring to a boil and simmer the mixture for 10 minutes. Strain it through a fine sieve into a bowl. Add gelatin mixture and lemon juice to tomato mixture and stir thoroughly while still hot until the gelatin is dissolved. Let cool for 15 minutes.

Lightly oil a fluted 1¼-quart crown-shaped mold and wipe so only a fine film remains. Pour tomato mixture in, cool, and chill until firm (about 4 hours). When ready to unmold, set the mold in hot water a few seconds, run a knife around the edge, invert a serving plate over the mold, and invert the mold onto it. Serves 6 to 8.

PICKLED BEETS

4 cups cooked beets	2 teaspoons uniodized salt
2 cups apple cider vinegar	1 teaspoon whole cloves
1 cup sugar	

Scrub medium-size or small beets. Cut stems to 1 inch and boil until tender, then drain. When beets are cool enough to handle, peel off the skins, cut off stems, and slice to ¼ inch.

In a heavy stainless steel saucepan, combine all other ingredients, bring the mixture to a boil, and stir until the sugar is dissolved, then add beets. Simmer for 5 minutes, transfer to a bowl, and let cool. Beets may be chilled in the pickling brine for several hours and served immediately or canned.

Pack beets in hot sterilized pint jars, cover with brine to ½ inch of the top of the can, and seal. Makes 2 pints.

PIONEER PUMPKIN PIE

My mother and Ingeborg often made pumpkin pie for the winter holidays. This recipe has a mild yet rich taste.

For the 9-inch unbaked pie shell: use recipe for Carrine's Flaky Pie Crust (see page 23)	*1 tablespoon melted butter or margarine*
For the filling:	*½ teaspoon cinnamon*
1 cup canned or fresh pumpkin	*¼ teaspoon ginger*
⅔ cup light brown sugar	*¼ teaspoon nutmeg*
1 teaspoon dark molasses	*½ teaspoon salt*
2 large eggs	*1¼ cups light cream*
	whipping cream (for topping)

After making pie shell, refrigerate for 30 minutes. Place pumpkin, brown sugar, and molasses in a large mixing bowl and combine well. (If using fresh pumpkin, boil well until tender, drain, and mash very well—if pumpkin still looks rough, put in the blender a minute.) In a small bowl combine eggs, melted butter, spices, and salt and beat well with an eggbeater. Pour over pumpkin mixture and add cream and stir until smooth. Pour into refrigerated shell.

Pumpkin pie is best if baked at a long slow heat—pumpkin filling that has been allowed to boil in the oven is not palatable. Start out at 400 degrees for 10 to 12 minutes and then lower heat to 300 degrees and bake for up to another hour or until a knife inserted in the filling comes out clean. Cool pie on rack until warm and serve with a liberal topping of freshly whipped cream sweetened with a little sugar and vanilla. Serves 8.

PEPPARKAKOR
(Swedish Gingersnaps)

These crisp, tangy cookies are a delight for children at Christmas or Thanksgiving. Cookie cutters in the shape of Christmas trees, Santas, reindeer, bells, or turkeys and pilgrims can be used.

½ cup butter or margarine	1 teaspoon soda
⅔ cup firmly packed light brown sugar	½ teaspoon cinnamon
	½ teaspoon nutmeg
1 teaspoon vanilla	½ teaspoon ginger
1 large egg, beaten lightly	¼ teaspoon ground cloves
1¾ cups all-purpose flour	½ teaspoon salt

In a bowl with an electric mixer beat butter, sugar, and vanilla until smooth, add beaten egg, then flour that has been sifted with soda, spices, and salt. Wrap dough well in floured waxed paper and chill overnight or at least 6 hours.

Because of the brown sugar content, chilled dough will be hard. Cut dough into four batches for rolling, keeping the unrolled batches in the refrigerator until needed.

Crumble each quarter of dough to soften slightly, then press together again, making a smooth ball. Roll out very thin on a floured pastry cloth to ¹⁄₁₆ inch thick. Cut with lightly floured cookie cutters into various shapes and transfer to lightly buttered cookie sheets with a spatula. Make cookies with the remaining dough in the same manner, rolling out the scraps last. Bake at 350 degrees on an upper rack of oven for 6 to 8 minutes until golden at the edges. Let cookies cool on racks and store in airtight tins. Makes at least 6 dozen.

MYRTLE'S *SANDBAKKELS*
(Butter Tarts)

Fluted tins (3 inches in diameter at the top and 1 inch high) are necessary to make these beautiful, cup-shaped Christmas cookies, which can be served alone, inverted on a plate, or filled with ice cream, whipped cream, lemon filling, or lingonberry preserves. Do not save this recipe for a rainy day: dry weather makes the dough much easier to work with.

1 cup butter	*1 teaspoon almond extract*
1 cup margarine (or lard or shortening)	*1 large beaten egg*
	4½ cups all-purpose flour
2 cups sugar	*½ teaspoon salt*

In a large bowl blend together sugar, butter, citrus juices, and peels well with electric mixer, add egg yolk, vanilla, and almond extract until well combined. With a spoon, blend in flour sifted with salt thoroughly and add nuts.
in half, and form two rolls about 9 × 2½ inches. Wrap well in lightly floured waxed paper and chill at least several hours or overnight.

When dough is firm, slice the rolls in circles to ⅛ inch thick and press into the *sandbakkel* tins to form shells about 1/16 inch thick, making the bottoms slightly thinner than the sides (the dough will settle a little in baking). To facilitate forming the shells, if desired, press the dough with another *sandbakkel* tin the same size which has been dipped in flour.

Arrange the tarts on a baking sheet about 1 inch apart and chill again until firm (15 to 30 minutes) before baking in a 350 degree oven for 10 to 12 minutes or until golden and slightly brown around the edges. Remove the tins, inverted, to a cooling rack. Cool until tins can be handled, then twirl in the hands and press in gently with the fingertips until tarts loosen, then invert carefully on the rack. Let the tarts cool completely before storing in airtight tins. Makes about 40 3-inch *sandbakkels*.

NORWEGIAN *SPRITZ*

Spritz could be called the signature Scandinavian cookie. They were my mother's favorite cookie because the dough is so versatile and can be put in a cookie press to make all the traditional Scandinavian shapes: the letter *s*, bows, circles, and ribbons. But she usually made them the easy way: pressing them with a fork to make a crosshatch pattern and sprinkling them with a combination of red and green sugar crystals for Christmas.

1½ cups butter or margarine (a combination of both is best)
1 cup sugar
1½ teaspoons vanilla
½ teaspoon almond extract
1 medium egg
4 cups flour
½ teaspoon baking powder
½ teaspoon salt

Cream butter, sugar, vanilla, and almond extract together, add egg, then flour that has been sifted with the other dry ingredients, and combine well. Form dough in balls the size of a small walnut and place several inches apart on ungreased cookie sheets. Flatten gently with the tines of a floured fork, pressing first one way and then the other, to about 1¾ inches in diameter. Bake at 325 degrees for 12 to 15 minutes until a golden yellow and slightly brown around the edges. Cool on racks and store in airtight tins. Makes about 6 dozen.

CITRUS COOKIES

These Christmas cookies are wonderfully redolent of lemon and orange.

¾ cup light brown sugar
1 cup butter or margarine
½ teaspoon orange juice
½ teaspoon lemon juice
½ teaspoon grated orange peel
½ teaspoon grated lemon peel

1 large egg yolk
½ teaspoon vanilla
¼ teaspoon almond extract
2½ cups sifted flour
¼ teaspoon salt
¾ cup chopped nuts
1 slightly beaten egg white (for glaze)

In a large bowl blend together sugar, butter, citrus juices, and peels well with electric mixer, add egg yolk, vanilla, and almond extract until well combined. With a spoon, blend in flour sifted with salt thoroughly and add nuts.

Flour the hands and form dough into balls slightly bigger than a walnut. Flatten balls somewhat in the palm of the hand and dip the tops of cookies in the egg white before placing on greased cookie sheets. Bake at 350 degrees for about 12 minutes until golden. Makes 3 dozen.

BERLINERKRANSER
(Christmas Wreaths)

My mother's sister-in-law, Anna, shared with us this recipe for *berlinerkranser*, which she had brought from Gudbransdal, Norway. Anna came to the North Dakota prairie to keep house for my bachelor uncle, Ole, on his homestead and soon married him. She never learned to speak English, taking the position that, surrounded by people willing and able to address her in her native tongue, who needed it?

2 hard-boiled large egg yolks (well mashed or sieved)

2 large raw egg yolks (lightly beaten)

¾ cup butter or margarine (a combination of both is best)

1 cup powdered sugar

2 cups flour

1 large egg white (lightly beaten, for glaze)

½ cup lump sugar (coarsely crushed)

In a small bowl combine the hard-boiled egg yolks and the raw egg yolks until the mixture is smooth. In a mixing bowl cream the butter and sugar together until it is light and fluffy, add the egg yolk mixture, and combine well. Add the flour and mix well to form a stiff dough. Halve the dough, wrap each half in floured waxed paper, and chill at least 1 hour or until it is firm.

Work with only one-fourth of the dough at a time out of the refrigerator. Pinch off walnut-size pieces of dough and, on a lightly floured working surface with floured hands, roll them into ½-inch-thick ropes about 4½ inches in length. Cross the ends of each length to form a loop or *e* shape and dip the tops (one side only) first in the lightly beaten egg white and then in the crushed lump sugar. Place 2 inches apart on lightly buttered baking sheets and bake in a moderately slow oven (300 to 325 degrees) for 15 to 20 minutes or until they are light golden on top and light brown around the edges. Transfer to racks to cool and store in airtight tins—they keep very well for three or four days. Makes about 4 dozen.

A Note on the Recipes

Compiling these recipes was both a rewarding and a challenging experience. At times I felt as exhilarated as an archaeologist on a successful dig. Some recipes were found, written in almost indecipherable faded ink, without instructions or oven temperatures included. A few were discovered in the bottoms of old recipe boxes without lids and tried for the first time. What a pleasure (and a relief) it was when they turned out well. The delectable Whipped Cream Cake is an example. Others I had made all my life, such as my favorite Christmas cookies *spritz* and *berlinerkranser*. Several recipes were only a well-remembered taste of my mother's and had to be recreated until memory and reality became one. My aunts, always generous with their recipes over the years, were responsible for many fine ones. My grandmother's legacy has sifted down.

Our grandmothers, of course, didn't have modern conveniences or appliances, only cookstoves that didn't bake evenly. A dozen egg whites for an angel food cake had to be beaten up entirely by hand with a wire whisk or an eggbeater. Every kitchen utensil had at least two uses, and nothing must go to waste. Foods were kept without refrigeration on the cold floor of the cellar during the hot summers; milk, butter, and eggs were used quickly. Fruits and vegetables were canned against the long winters.

We have tried to avoid unnecessary modernizing of recipes. With our cholesterol-conscious society in mind, we have found that a 100-percent corn-oil margarine can almost always successfully be substituted for butter, with this exception: when greasing waxed paper under cake batter, butter should be used. For Christmas cookies where a richer taste is preferred, half butter and half margarine is a good compromise. Recipes were tested using 2 percent milk. Insulated cookie sheets will benefit all of the cookie recipes, insuring even baking and reducing the chance of overbrowning.

Whatever your ancestry or cooking traditions, write down your favorite recipes; they are your children's heritage. And let your young children or grandchildren "experiment" in the kitchen. I recall making my first cake, a small version of devil's food, at age seven, with only my paternal grandmother sitting close by to monitor my turning the oven on and off correctly. What a wonderful memory!

—Felicia Young

Recipe Index

Bur Oak Books

A Cook's Tour of Iowa
By Susan Puckett

The Folks
By Ruth Suckow

Fragile Giants: A Natural History of the Loess Hills
By Cornelia F. Mutel

An Iowa Album: A Photographic History, 1860–1920
By Mary Bennett

Iowa Birdlife
By Gladys Black

Landforms of Iowa
By Jean C. Prior

More han Ola og han Per
By Peter J. Rosendahl

Neighboring on the Air: Cooking with the KMA Radio Homemakers
By Evelyn Birkby

Nineteenth Century Home Architecture of Iowa City: A Silver Anniversary Edition
By Margaret N. Keyes

Nothing to Do but Stay: My Pioneer Mother
By Carrie Young

Old Capitol: Portrait of an Iowa Landmark
By Margaret N. Keyes

Parsnips in the Snow: Talks with Midwestern Gardeners
By Jane Anne Staw and Mary Swander

A Place of Sense: Essays in Search of the Midwest
Edited by Michael Martone

Prairie Cooks: Glorified Rice, Three-Day Buns, and Other Reminiscences
By Carrie Young with Felicia Young

Prairies, Forests, and Wetlands: The Restoration of Natural Landscape Communities in Iowa
By Janette R. Thompson

A Ruth Suckow Omnibus
By Ruth Suckow

"A Secret to Be Burried": The Diary and Life of Emily Hawley Gillespie, 1858–1888
By Judy Nolte Lensink